My Personal
Daily Prayer Book

CHRISTINE A. DALLMAN
MARGARET ANNE HUFFMAN

Publications International, Ltd.

CHRISTINE A. DALLMAN is a freelance writer who has contributed to the devotional publication *The Quiet Hour* and is a former editor and columnist for *Sunday Digest* magazine. She is the author of *Daily Devotions for Seniors*, an inspirational resource for maturing adults, as well as coauthor of *How to Let God Help You Through Hard Times*.

MARGARET ANNE HUFFMAN is an award-winning journalist and former lifestyle editor of the *Shelby News*. She has written and contributed to many books, including *Simple Wisdom, A Moment With God for Mothers,* and *Everyday Prayers for Grandmothers*.

Louis Weber, CEO
Publications International, Ltd.
7373 North Cicero Avenue
Lincolnwood, Illinois 60712

ISBN-13: 978-1-4127-1372-6
ISBN-10: 1-4127-1372-2

Manufactured in China.

8 7 6 5 4 3 2 1

Library of Congress Control: 2006903676

Talking With God 🐚

*I*MAGINE IF YOU HAD a direct channel to the Creator of the universe. Imagine if you could just speak to him, and he would hear you. More than that, he would listen. What would you say? Whatever you say, this is prayer.

Aside from listening to God's messages to us, there may be no greater opportunity available to us than talking directly to God through prayer. It's evidence of his great love for his children that he accepts our "please's" and "thank-you's" and "hallelujah's"—and actively responds to them.

It's also evidence of our faith that we approach him in prayer. We don't talk with someone who isn't there. And the more we talk, the more we realize that God works in us through those conversations far beyond the requests we bring. He uses our prayers to draw us closer to him, helping us see him more clearly.

This book of daily prayers is specifically designed as an enjoyable tool to be used by those who talk with God. It includes prayers—both formal and informal, classic and modern—on a wide variety of subjects. Some days feature prayers of thanksgiving; other days offer requests for God's guidance; and still others will lead you in prayers of praise to God for his grace, mercy, or creative genius. In addition to the daily prayer, most days will also include a brief passage from Scripture and an inspirational quote.

None of the prayers in this collection are more acceptable or effective than any sincere communication from one of God's children. They are simply offered as a starting place. Each can be prayed word-for-word or used as a blueprint for your own prayers. Our hope is that you will make these prayers your own as you personally talk with God.

At the end of each month, you will find a blank page entitled "My Prayer Life." This space has been set aside for you to write specific requests, items of praise and thanks, or notes about what God is teaching you through prayer and his Word from the past month. This is where you can compose your own prayers.

Our hope is that this book will help you take a fuller opportunity of the awesome privilege of talking with God every day.

*The spirit of the Lord God...has sent me to bring good
news...to proclaim the year of the Lord's favor.*

ISAIAH 61:1–2

$\mathcal{G}$OD, a new year brings a sense of fresh-
ness, of possibilities for the future, and of
discoveries yet to be made. I look forward
to stepping into the days ahead, knowing
that you will guide me into the good
purposes you have planned for my life. I
ask you for an extra measure of courage,
strength, optimism, and faith to meet
every challenge along the way.

January 2

For with you is the fountain of life; in your light we see light.

PSALM 36:9

GOD, you have blessed me with yet another year during which to grow. You have also blessed me with the opportunity to realize the potential you have placed within my life. Thank you for each of the past years, for in them you have taught me more and more how to embrace truth and nurture love. I can't count the number of times I've returned to your wellspring of wisdom to gain insight into and understanding of my life. Thank you for your guidance. Please, lead me into today with an open heart and mind, ready to learn still more. Amen.

Lord, you have been our dwelling place in all generations.
PSALM 90:1

LORD, you are my home where I can return and get my bearings in a crazy world. When I feel lost or homeless and my spirit drifts toward the jagged edges of my problems, help me remember to turn to you for help, for in you there is rescue, refuge, and peace. I thank you that there is always a place for me in your heart.

O God, our help in ages past,
Our hope for years to come,
Our shelter from the stormy blast,
And our eternal home.
—ISAAC WATTS, "O GOD, OUR HELP IN AGES PAST"

January 4

GOD, sometimes it's easy to think that winter is a season merely to endure until springtime ushers in the days of summer. But then, when I step outside on a calm winter's day, I find tiny wonders everywhere, tucked away like special treasures for the one who cares to seek them out. You have made winter a special season of rest and reflection, a time of discovering beauty against the backdrop of bleakness. Thank you for the exquisite blessings of winter.

Many of the phenomena of Winter are suggestive of an inexpressible tenderness and fragile delicacy. We are accustomed to hear this king described as a rude and boisterous tyrant; but with the gentleness of a lover he adorns the tresses of Summer.

—HENRY DAVID THOREAU, *WALDEN*

The Lord God helps me; therefore I have not been disgraced; therefore I have set my face like flint, and I know that I shall not be put to shame.

ISAIAH 50:7

*H*ELP ME, Lord, when I lack the will to reach for my dreams and when demands on my time interfere with the spiritual disciplines you've brought into my life. Help me keep them in sight and not waste my energies focusing on past failures. Help me throw my entire self— mind, body, emotions—into gaining the victory. For with your help, I *can* win!

Obstacles cannot crush me
Every obstacle yields to stern resolve
he who is fixed to a star does not change his mind.
—LEONARDO DA VINCI

January 6

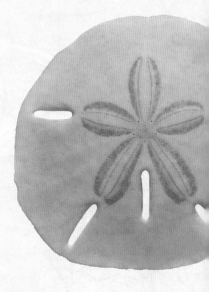

You have turned my mourning into dancing;...and clothed me with joy.

PSALM 30:11

GREAT IS, O King,
our happiness
in thy kingdom,
thou, our king....

May our feet
be made strong;
let us dance before thee,
eternal....

—"GREAT IS OUR HAPPINESS"

One time when I was a child, my dad and uncle were playing their guitars together. The music called out my joy, and I began to somersault and dance with no thought of anything or anyone else. Of all the human expressions of joy, dancing is perhaps the most delightful and complete. During a moment of alone time, invite your joy to come out of hiding by turning up your favorite music and dancing with abandon.

January 7

> *But I trust in you, O Lord;…My times are in your hand.*
> PSALM 31:14–15

*D*EAR HEAVENLY FATHER, life is full of surprises: a mixed bag, the good and the bad. Of course, we welcome the good, but when the bad befalls us, we seek reasons for and relief from it. As much as we try to avoid distasteful and hurtful circumstances, Lord, it is often in these that we realize how significant and meaningful our faith is. As a result, we pray that you will teach us to always reach out to you. Amen.

January 8

Deceit is in the mind of those who plan evil, but those who counsel peace have joy.

PROVERBS 12:20

ALMIGHTY GOD, from who all thoughts of truth and peace proceed, kindle we pray Thee, in the hearts of all men the true love of peace.... Amen.

—FRANCIS PAGET

In a world of high stress and short tempers, peacemakers stand out in a crowd. People notice when we choose kindness rather than retribution. They wonder at us when we use a soft word instead of an angry one in a tense situation. But peacemakers are not wimps: They exercise amazing self-control when they reject impulsive words and behavior in order to promote peace.

January 9 🐚

*T*ODAY, LORD, don't let my day pass without savoring one or more of the following: the feeling of a hug or smile from someone I love; the sights of creation from flowers, trees, and animals to a sunset or moon rise; the taste of a favorite flavor or smell; the sound of a song I enjoy singing or listening to; the sense of accomplishment I feel from a job well done; the uniqueness of this day you've given to me.

January 10

As a father has compassion for his children, so the Lord has compassion for those who fear him. For he knows how we were made; he remembers that we are dust.

PSALM 103:13–14

DEAR GOD, be good to
me. The sea is so wide,
and my boat is so small.
—"THE BRETON FISHERMAN'S PRAYER"

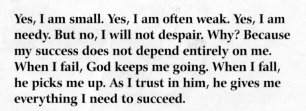

**Yes, I am small. Yes, I am often weak. Yes, I am
needy. But no, I will not despair. Why? Because
my success does not depend entirely on me.
When I fail, God keeps me going. When I fall,
he picks me up. As I trust in him, he gives me
everything I need to succeed.**

January 11

*Two are better than one, because they have a good reward
for their toil. For if they fall, one will lift up the other.*

ECCLESIASTES 4:9–10

THE WIRES ARE holding hands around the holes:
To avoid breaking the ring, they hold tight the
  neighbouring wrist,
And it's thus that with holes they make a fence.

Lord, there are lots of holes in my life.
There are some in the lives of my neighbours.
But if you wish we shall hold hands
We shall hold very tight
And together we shall make a roll of fence to adorn
  Paradise.

—MICHEL QUOIST, "THE WIRE FENCE"

**God's gift of community is a
beautiful and purposeful
design of interdependence–
of helping and being helped.
Since it is a gift, however,
community will never happen
unless we first reach out to
receive it.**

January 12

*To get wisdom is to love oneself; to
keep understanding is to prosper.*
PROVERBS 19:8

LORD, I want so much to do the right thing, to have the
right answers, and to be the right kind of person. Yet, so
often I feel as though I'm doing things all wrong, looking
for answers that don't exist, and being just the kind of
person I can't stand! Then things are made worse
because I get all wound around myself, focusing on my
failure and getting discouraged. Please help me unwind
and refocus on the simple facts that you made me and
you love me and you are in the process of making me all
I need to be. Thanks for sticking with me. Amen.

I can do all things through him who strengthens me.

PHILIPPIANS 4:13

CHRIST BE WITH ME, Christ within me,
Christ behind me, Christ before me,
Christ beside me, Christ to win me,
Christ to comfort me and restore me.
Christ beneath me, Christ above me.
Christ in quiet, Christ in danger,
Christ in hearts of all who love me,
Christ in mouth of friend or stranger.

—ST. PATRICK

As we learn to trust Christ, we discover his strengthening
presence in various places and people. Wherever we encounter
shelter, comfort, rest, and peace, we are bound to hear his voice
welcoming us there. And in whomever we find truth, love,
gentleness, and humility we are sure to hear his heartbeat,
assuring us that he will always be near.

January 14

Anxiety weighs down the human heart, but a good word cheers it up.
PROVERBS 12:25

FATHER, may I seldom speak a discouraging word. Check my negative thoughts and focus on the positive things in others. Fill my lips with sincere and authentic praise that will encourage their hearts and give them the ability to rise above any obstacles that may be bringing them down.

The beautiful part about encouragement is this: Anybody can do it. You don't need a lot of money to carry it out. You don't even need to be a certain age. In fact, some of the most encouraging actions or words I've received have come from my own children.
—CHARLES R. SWINDOLL, *STRENGTHENING YOUR GRIP*

January 15

> *You have heard that it was said, "You shall love your neighbor and hate your enemy." But I say to you, Love your enemies and pray for those who persecute you, so that you may be children of your Father in heaven.*
>
> MATTHEW 5:43–45

*I*N A WORLD divided by color bars, how sweet a thing it is to know that in thee we all belong to one family.…Help us, O God, to refuse to be embittered against those who handle us with harshness.…Save us from hatred of those who oppress us.…May we follow the spirit of thy Son Jesus Christ.

—BANTU, "ONE FAMILY"

Our enemies may not want our love, but they desperately need it. Hatred is deadly to the soul and is cured only with the antidote of reconciling love. When we extend this kind of love to our enemies, we not only purge our own hearts of their poison but also offer hope to those who are slowly dying from the toxic effects of hatred.

January 16

Happy are those who consider the poor; the Lord delivers them in the day of trouble. The Lord protects them and keeps them alive; they are called happy in the land.

PSALM 41:1–2

*L*ORD, when I consider all the war, hunger, oppression, and homelessness in my world, I feel overwhelmed and insignificant, unable to think of how my small resources could begin to touch the great need I've been made aware of. Remind me, Father, that if each person with his or her tiny bit of energy, time, and money would meet a need nearby, then a great deal of suffering could be alleviated by people just like me. I guess it's time for me to ask you to challenge my faith in this truth by showing me a need nearby.

I never think in terms of crowds in general but in terms of persons. Were I to think about crowds, I would never begin anything. It is the person that matters. I believe in person-to-person encounters.

—MOTHER TERESA, *HEART OF JOY*

*The Lord bless you and keep you; the Lord make his face
to shine upon you, and be gracious to you; the Lord lift up
his countenance upon you, and give you peace.*

Numbers 6:24–26

*F*ATHER IN HEAVEN!
When the thought of thee
wakes in our hearts let it
not awaken like a fright-
ened bird that flies about
in dismay, but like a child
waking from its sleep with
a heavenly smile.

—Søren Kierkegaard

**For God's children, the biblical expression "fear God" has nothing
to do with being frightened of God, as one might be frightened
of a goblin or a ferocious animal. No, the fear we are instructed
to have of God is more akin to the emotions we feel in the presence of a person we greatly respect, admire, even worship. It is
at once a feeling of deep humility and of exquisite honor.**

January 18

God, I know that integrity means being the same on the outside as on the inside, in public as in private, in my heart as in my actions. Sometimes I feel the friction between these realms as I try to build an image apart from reality. Please save me from the temptations of half-truths, pretense, and inauthenticity. Help me do the hard work of bringing my character in line with what I want it to be, instead of taking the shortcut of creating a false persona. Today I'll start with the little things, God. Help me be faithful in them so that I'll be strong enough to stand when the big tests of my character come along.

It is necessary to the happiness of man that he be mentally faithful to himself.
—Thomas Paine, *The Age of Reason*

January 19

*Let all who take refuge in you rejoice;
let them ever sing for joy. Spread your
protection over them, so that those who
love your name may exult in you.*

PSALM 5:11

*A*BIDE WITH ME—fast falls the eventide;
The darkness deepens—Lord, with me abide!
When other helpers fail and comforts flee,
Help of the helpless, oh, abide with me!

—HENRY F. LYTE, "ABIDE WITH ME"

**If I believed there were no God, the depth of my loneliness and
despair would be inconsolable. But I know God is real, for he has
always consoled me when I have felt loneliness or despair. Today,
allow God to comfort and console the most vulnerable, hurting
places in your heart. Tell him all about it. He's there for you.**

January 20

Those who are attentive to a matter will prosper, and happy are those who trust in the Lord.

PROVERBS 16:20

$\mathcal{H}$EAVENLY FATHER, you have given me skills and relationships for the purpose of learning, growing, enjoying life, and finding fulfillment. Sometimes I feel the need to evaluate how I'm doing, to determine whether or not I'm accomplishing those purposes.

As I evaluate, please give me the courage and wisdom to know how to weed out the activities and relationships that threaten to choke the spiritual life out of me. Grant me the self-discipline to change habits and thought patterns that tear down what you are trying to build up in me. May I succeed in your strength and bring honor to you in all I do. Amen.

God has said, "I will never leave you or forsake you." So we can say with confidence, "The Lord is my helper; I will not be afraid. What can anyone do to me?"

HEBREWS 13:5–6

O LORD! thou knowest how busy I must be this day: if I forget thee, do not thou forget me.

—SIR JACOB ASTLEY

It is often said that life is a battle, and it's true that from day to day in our external world, we must fight our way through any number of difficult interactions, pesky interruptions, and trying irritations. But in the heat of the battle, whether we find ourselves in a good position or a bad one, we can be sure of this: God is there for us. At no point in these skirmishes will he ever turn his back on us or retreat from us. He is committed to helping us win the day, even when we forget he is there at all. However, before taking to the spiritual, emotional, and mental trenches of a new day, we would do well to take a moment to call on God and thank him for his faithful support.

January 22

The apostles gathered around Jesus, and told him all that they had done and taught. He said to them, "Come away to a deserted place all by yourselves and rest a while."

MARK 6:30–31

GOD, sometimes I am so caught up in my work that I become fragmented, exhausting myself and those around me. At these times, when I beg you for a miraculous infusion of strength, remind me that the miracle I seek can be accomplished in a very practical way—by resting. Help me to plan a time of rest today, Lord, a moment when I can steal away with you and be refreshed. Please bless my rest, I pray, and show me how to immerse myself in it and be made strong and whole again. Amen.

January 23

The Lord is near. Do not worry about anything, but in everything by prayer and supplication with thanksgiving let your requests be made known to God. And the peace of God, which surpasses all understanding, will guard your hearts and your minds in Christ Jesus.

PHILIPPIANS 4:5–7

*G*OD GIVE US GRACE to accept with serenity the things that cannot be changed, courage to change the things that should be changed, and wisdom to distinguish the one from the other.

—REINHOLD NIEBUHR

Trying to discern which things in life we should learn to accept and which things we should take initiative to change can create anxiety in our hearts and minds. But, of course, worry is futile and counterproductive in our quest for peace. Since only God's wisdom is adequate to give us the answers we need, we must be purposeful in abandoning our tendency to worry and, instead, become serious about asking God for the insight we need. Today, let his peace guard your heart and mind even while you bring your questions and requests to him.

January 24

*All to whom God ... enables to enjoy [life's riches],
and to accept their lot and find enjoyment in their
toil—this is the gift of God. For they will scarcely
brood over the days of their lives, because God
keeps them occupied with the joy of their hearts.*

ECCLESIASTES 5:19–20

You HAVE GRANTED, Lord, for me to find
enjoyment in relationships and in a myr-
iad of other fun and interesting things life
offers. Teach me to keep these pleasures
pure and alive by avoiding the extremes
of overindulgence and neglect. Thank you
for the moments of happiness that have
come to me as I have been able to lay
aside the heaviness that life can sometimes be and dive into the joy of spending time with the people and the
activities I love most.

January 25

*Thanks be to God, who in Christ
always leads us in triumphal
procession, and through us spreads
in every place the fragrance that
comes from knowing him.*

2 CORINTHIANS 2:14

*H*ELP ME to spread your fragrance everywhere I go—let me preach you without
preaching, not by words but by my example—
by the catching force, the sympathetic influence of what I do, the evident fullness of the
love my heart bears to you.

—JOHN HENRY NEWMAN, *THE FRAGRANCE OF CHRIST*

I can smell the soft, fresh scent of her perfume wherever she is.
This friend of mine doesn't have to say a word, for her presence
is known already. People often comment on how nice she smells.
Her lingering fragrance is her sensory hallmark. And as I consider
this, I wonder, is it possible for my life to have the lingering
fragrance of love? For my presence to bear a distinctive spiritual
scent by which others are influenced and to which they are
drawn? For sincere love to be the hallmark of my existence? May
it always be so!

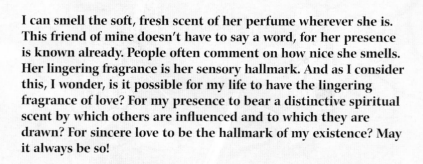

January 26

*So then, putting away falsehood, let all of
us speak the truth to our neighbors, for
we are members of one another.*

EPHESIANS 4:25

LORD, when those dearest to my heart are moving in
ill-advised directions, I feel compelled to speak up and
cry out "Danger!" But at the same time, I'm afraid my
loving intentions will be mistaken for meddling, for
opinionated attempts at control. I cannot bear to keep
silent, yet I cannot bear the thought of being shut out
and rejected by someone about whom I care so deeply.
But when I weigh those two things, I know that not to
speak would be unloving. So help me to offer words of
grace and truth in a spirit of gentleness that reveal my
love and yours as well. Amen.

**I love you and, because I love you, I would
sooner have you hate me for telling you the
truth than adore me for telling you lies.**

—PIETRO ARETINO

January 27

*Do not judge by appearances, but
judge with right judgment.*

JOHN 7:24

*G*RANT ME, O Lord, to know what is worth
knowing, to love what is worth loving, to
praise what delights you most, to value what
is precious in your sight, to hate what is offen-
sive to you. Do not let me judge by what I see,
nor pass sentence according to what I hear,
but to judge rightly between things that differ, and above all to search out and to do what
pleases you, through Jesus Christ our Lord.

—THOMAS À KEMPIS

**We are often told that we should not judge, period.
However, while the Bible decries judgmental attitudes, it
actually instructs us to judge, but we are to be careful to
judge rightly. Judgmental attitudes are based in seeking
to justify oneself while condemning another. Judging
rightly entails seeking truth and the good of all.**

January 28

A fool takes no pleasure in understanding, but only in expressing personal opinion.

PROVERBS 18:2

LORD, to take the time to understand another person's perspective is one of the deepest forms of respect I can show them. Help me, today, make an effort to gain insight into the thoughts, experiences, and feelings of those who seem different from me and also those with whom I am at odds. Take away my fear of losing my long-held opinions and ideas. Help me remember that truth can stand on its own and that sometimes my thoughts must change to come in line with that truth.

The field cannot be well seen from within the field.

—RALPH WALDO EMERSON

I have learned to be content with whatever I have. I know what it is to have little, and I know what it is to have plenty. In any and all circumstances I have learned the secret of being well-fed and of going hungry, of having plenty and of being in need.

PHILIPPIANS 4:11–12

*W*HEN PEACE like a river attendeth my way,
When sorrows like sea billows roll,
Whatever my lot, Thou has taught me to say,
"It is well, it is well with my soul."

—HORATIO G. SPAFFORD, "IT IS WELL WITH MY SOUL"

Contentment grows up from a grateful heart. We may sometimes think to ourselves, *I'd be happy, if only* . . . However, some of the most discontent people are those who seem to have it all. Contentment begins, not in having that one more thing that eludes our grasp, but in becoming deeply thankful for the things that are already within our grasp.

January 30

Above all, maintain constant love for one another, for love covers a multitude of sins.
1 PETER 4:8

LORD, your forgiveness, based in your love for me, has transformed my life. I've experienced inner healing and freedom in knowing that you have wiped my slate clean and made me your friend. Help me become an extension of your love to those around me. Let healing happen as I apply the salve of your forgiveness to the wounds others carry and to the wounds they inflict on me. Please strengthen me today while I carry it out in your name. Amen.

The practice of forgiveness is our most impor-ant contribution to the healing of the world.
—MARIANNE WILLIAMSON, *A RETURN TO LOVE*

January 31

*When the Spirit of truth comes, he
will guide you into all truth.*

JOHN 16:13

*F*ROM THE cowardice that dare not face new truth
From the laziness that is contented with half truth
From the arrogance that thinks it knows all truth,
Good Lord, deliver me.

—A PRAYER FROM KENYA

**To receive truth, we must be willing to face the
frightening realities about ourselves that rebel
against the truth. This takes courage. To assim-
ilate the truth into our lives means that we
must roll up our sleeves and begin the arduous
task of changing what is wrong in our thoughts,
attitudes, and actions. This takes diligence.
Then, to walk in truth as God would have us do,
we must resist the tendency to become critical
and condemning of others who are still in the
truth-seeking process. This takes humility.**

🐚 *My prayer life:*

_____

_____

_____

_____

_____

_____

_____

_____

_____

_____

_____

_____

_____

February 1 🐚

From its chamber comes the whirlwind,
and cold from the scattering winds.

JOB 37:9

*G*OD OF DAYS, months, and seasons, thank you for this
time deep in winter when, after the excitement of holidays, we settle back into our routines and relish the
quiet. Thank you that right in the heart of this season we
take time to celebrate what is at the heart of every love-
filled relationship: your love. Help us keep warm with
the love that fills our families and friendships. Amen.

Here comes February, a little girl with her first
valentine, a red bow in her windblown hair, a
kiss waiting on her lips, a tantrum just back of
her laughter.

—HAL BORLAND, *SUNDIAL OF THE SEASONS*

February 2

O taste and see that the Lord is good;
happy are those who take refuge in him.

PSALM 34:8

*G*OD, YOU ARE INVISIBLE but not unseen. You reveal yourself in creation and demonstrate your kindness in a stranger's sincere smile. You are intangible but not unfelt. You caress our faces with the wind and embrace us in a friend's arms. We look for you today and feel your presence. Amen.

February 3 🐚

I … beg you to lead a life worthy of the calling to which you have been called, with all humility and gentleness, with patience, bearing with one another in love, making every effort to maintain the unity of the Spirit in the bond of peace.

EPHESIANS 4:1–3

*H*EAVENLY FATHER, I don't see eye to eye with people I see everyday. In fact, their ways of doing things often annoy me. Yet, you have placed them in my life to refine the way I relate to people. Help me focus, not on what causes me to dislike them, but on what makes them precious to you. That way, I can learn to value them as well.

In necessary things, unity; in disputed things, liberty; in all things, charity.
—VARIOUSLY ASCRIBED. THE FORMULATION WAS USED AS A MOTTO BY THE ENGLISH NONCONFORMIST CLERIC RICHARD BAXTER.

February 4

*O Lord, how manifold are your works! In
wisdom you have made them all; the
earth is full of your creatures.... May the
glory of the Lord endure forever; may the
Lord rejoice in his works.*

O GOD, we thank you for this earth, our home; for the
wide sky and the blessed sun, for the salt sea and the
running water, for the everlasting hills and the never-
resting winds, for trees and the common grass underfoot.
We thank you for our senses by which we hear the songs
of birds, and see the splendour of the summer fields, and
taste of the autumn fruits, and rejoice in the feel of snow,
and smell the breath of the spring. Grant us a heart wide
open to all this beauty; and save our souls from being so
blind that we pass unseeing when even the common
thornbush is aflame with your glory, O God our creator.

—WALTER RAUSCHENBUSCH

**Look out your window. List the beauty of nature visible to you,
even if it includes only the sky above. Open your window and
listen. What do you hear? What smells meet your senses? Can
you taste a raindrop? Catch a snowflake? Feel the sun's warmth?
They are all blessings from God to you.**

Mary… sat at the Lord's feet and listened to what he was saying. But Martha was distracted by her many tasks; so she came to [Jesus] and asked, "Lord, do you not care that my sister has left me to do all the work by myself? Tell her then to help me." But the Lord answered her, "Martha, Martha, you are worried and distracted by many things; there is need of only one thing. Mary has chosen the better part, which will not be taken away from her."

LUKE 10:39–42

JESUS, you know how to keep things simple. During your time on earth, you never let people complicate your life and distract you from your purpose. You knew when to go all out to help people. You knew when to take a break. You knew how to deal with your opponents without letting them drag you down. You knew how to be a good friend. You knew when it was time to go home and let others pick up where you left off. How did you do it? How did you know? Please show me. I'm ready to listen and learn. Amen.

The ability to simplify means to eliminate the unnecessary so that the necessary may speak.
—HANS HOFMANN, *SEARCH FOR THE REAL*

February 6

Do nothing from selfish ambition or conceit, but in humility regard others as better than yourselves. Let each of you look not to your own interests, but to the interests of others.

PHILIPPIANS 2:3–4

O GOD, you have bound us together in this bundle of life; give us grace to understand how our lives depend on the courage, the industry, the honesty and integrity of our fellow men; that we may be mindful of their needs, grateful for their faithfulness, and faithful in our responsibilities to them; through Jesus Christ our Lord.

—REINHOLD NIEBUHR

Appreciation lets others know that we do not take them for granted. Is there a person who comes to mind as someone whose presence in or contribution to your life has been a help or a blessing? A small gift, a card, even a word of thanks will let them know how much you value them and all they've done for you.

February 7

Do not adorn yourselves outwardly…by wearing gold ornaments or fine clothing; rather, let your adornment be the inner self with the lasting beauty of a gentle and quiet spirit, which is very precious in God's sight.

1 PETER 3:3–4

LORD, in this culture of superficial standards of beauty, standards which I, too, am prone to adopt, keep me free from the foolish practice of ascribing value to strangers on the basis of their looks. Remind me of friends in my life whose appearance might be described as plain but who are exquisitely beautiful to me. Help me, God, not to regard my own looks as a basis for merit or lack of merit. Remind me to look within myself and cultivate true beauty in my heart.

The tulip and the butterfly
Appear in gayer coats than I:
Let me be dressed fine as I will,
Flies, worms, and flowers exceed me still.
—ISAAC WATTS, "AGAINST PRIDE IN CLOTHES"

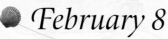

February 8

*Be filled with the Spirit, as you sing
psalms and hymns and spiritual songs
among yourselves, singing and making
melody to the Lord in your hearts.*

EPHESIANS 5:18–19

THERE SEEMS TO BE a song for every occasion, heavenly
Father. Life experiences inspire songs in us and beckon
us to sing. When I think of you, God, it is no exception;
there is a song that rises up as well. Sometimes that song
is a call for help, sometimes a shout for joy, still other
times it is a love song. Singing to you about what is in
my soul remains for me a special means of connection to
you for which I am grateful. Amen.

**Singing is in a line of descent from the psalms,
a way of puncturing reality, the ordered
structure of things as they are. As soon as we
start to sing, dance, remember, things are not
as they are. We are no longer just gathering in
the hay, as it were. It's a weird thing to do—a
non-animal-like thing to do. The angel in us.**
—DENNIS POTTER, SERIALS WITH SONGS

Jesus was praying in a certain place, and after he had finished, one of his disciples said to him, "Lord, teach us to pray."

LUKE 11:1

OUR FATHER IN HEAVEN, hallowed be your name. Your kingdom come. Your will be done, on earth as it is in heaven. Give us this day our daily bread. And forgive us our debts, as we also have forgiven our debtors. And do not bring us to the time of trial, but rescue us from the evil one.

—JESUS (MATTHEW 6:9–13)

Jesus' disciples recognized a connection between prayer and the special relationship Jesus had with his heavenly Father. Apparently they wanted to have that kind of closeness with God, too, so they asked Jesus to instruct them in prayer. The brevity and simplicity of that prayer is delightful. At the same time, this prayer contains all the elements for maintaining a strong relationship, such as respect and appropriate expressions of personal interests and concerns. So, open up and pray. God would enjoy talking with you today.

February 10

*Ask, and it will be given you; search, and you will find;
knock, and the door will be opened for you.*

MATTHEW 7:7

MY MIND, O God, is thirsty to know
you, to know myself, and to know my
world, but there is only so much time in a
day. Lead me into the learning that will be
most productive and helpful in accomplishing your purposes for myself and
others. Teach me to wisely manage the
knowledge that you have given me, never
using it to tear others down or to wrongly
lift myself up. And thank you for the
ability to discover, learn, and expand my
understanding. Please bless my quest for
truth by leading me to it.

**Curiosity is one of the most
permanent and certain
characteristics of a vigorous
intellect.**

—SAMUEL JOHNSON, *RAMBLER*

February 11

Have you not known? Have you not heard? The Lord is the everlasting God, the Creator of the ends of the earth. He does not faint or grow weary; his understanding is unsearchable. He gives power to the faint, and strengthens the powerless.

ISAIAH 40:28–29

DEAR LORD, there is an unsolvable problem staring me in the face right now—a Goliath-size impossibility shouting insults at me. Help me look away from the problem long enough to look at you and remember again just who you are. It's true that as long as I'm trying to solve the problem on my own, it will remain unsolved. I'm helpless to manage it because it is far bigger than I am. And yet, I know that you are bigger than my problem, because nothing is bigger than you. No one is stronger. When I call on you to replace me as my problem solver, you take over. And that's when Goliath falls and my problem gets cut down to size … and all this as the wheels of the galaxies continue to spin. Amen.

February 12

SOMETIMES temporary chaos is unavoidable, heavenly Father, and I'm OK with that reality. But I'd like my life, on a normal day, to be characterized by the kind of order that brings a sense of rest and peace. It's the kind of order that minimizes wastefulness and maximizes the amount of quality time I can spend doing things I enjoy and being with people I love. I want the pieces of my life to have their place, to fit together, and to make sense—to have purpose and meaning. I see order in the natural world and understand it is part of your design for the universe. Thank you for your example in this. Teach me to emulate you.

**Order marches with weighty and measured
strides; disorder is always in a hurry.**
—NAPOLEON BONAPARTE

February 13

Sing for joy, O heavens, and exult, O earth; break forth, O mountains, into singing! For the Lord has comforted his people, and will have compassion on his suffering ones.

ISAIAH 49:13

JOYFUL, JOYFUL, we adore Thee,
God of glory, Lord of love;
Hearts unfold like flowers before Thee,
Opening to the sun above.
Melt the clouds of sin and sadness,
Drive the dark of doubt away;
Giver of immortal gladness,
Fill us with the light of day.

—HENRY VAN DYKE

Wintertime seems to be the peak season for funks of all colors. Some winters I've been through a rainbow of funks, but I have found a secret for beating them back. I listen to inspirational music that's quiet and sympathizes with my mood, and then I move on to upbeat songs. If your funk is persistent, you may not beat it this way, but you might just get a little vacation from it.

February 14

Just as water reflects the face, so one human heart reflects another.

PROVERBS 27:19

$\mathcal{G}$OD, I remember the day I met the love of my life. As our relationship developed, I could scarcely believe that there was even more to discover about one another. In fact, we were also alike in many intriguing ways. I am convinced that your love is reflected through our love. I am truly privileged to have such a special relationship. Thank you, God.

Recognizing the matching essence in each other, like a single breath–separate, distinctive, and yet of the same essence–is what unites our hearts into a bond.

February 15

I urge that supplications, prayers, intercessions, and thanksgivings be made for everyone, for kings and all who are in high positions, so that we may lead a quiet and peaceable life in all godliness and dignity. This is right and is acceptable in the sight of God.

1 TIMOTHY 2:1–3

ℛEGARDLESS of who I voted for, Lord, the person who is in office is leading now. So what's the best course of action for me? Well, until the next election, it's simply to pray. Pray that the individual will be your instrument for bringing good to society. Pray that you will give this person wisdom and insight beyond the scope of partisan interests. Pray that, during this leader's term, you will maintain peace and increase righteousness throughout the land. Amen.

February 16

> *Then Peter began to curse, and he swore an oath, "I do not know the man!" At that moment the cock crowed. Then Peter remembered what Jesus had said: "Before the cock crows, you will deny me three times." And Peter went out and wept bitterly.*
>
> MATTHEW 26:74–75

IN ME there is darkness,
But with thee there is light,
I am lonely, but thou leavest me not.
I am feeble in heart, but thou leavest me not.
I am restless, but with thee there is peace.
In me there is bitterness, but with thee there is patience;
Thy ways are past understanding, but
Thou knowest the way for me.

—DIETRICH BONHOEFFER

Failure, painful as it is, does not end the possibility of success. Rather, failure is perhaps the most fertile ground in which true success may grow up. Failure checks our pride, helps us become willing to submit our ambitions to honest scrutiny, and gives us the ability to succeed with grace. Jesus gave Simon the name Peter long before the impetuous disciple lived up to his given name. Ironically, it wasn't until after Peter's great failure that he succeeded in becoming Peter "the rock."

February 17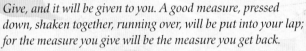

Give, and it will be given to you. A good measure, pressed down, shaken together, running over, will be put into your lap; for the measure you give will be the measure you get back.

LUKE 6:38

SOMETIMES IT SEEMS all backward, Lord. Is the way to experience true security by being generous with what we have? It is, for I know that all I have, you've given me, even the strength and ability to achieve and earn. You've provided for my needs from your limitless reserve of resources, so for me to give to others is really not to deplete anything at all. It is merely a joyful distribution of your riches. Please continue to teach me to trust you and to love others through abundant giving.

A man of humanity is one who, in seeking to establish himself, finds a foothold for others and who, desiring attainment for himself, helps others to attain.

—CONFUCIUS

February 18

The earth is the Lord's and all that is in it, the world, and those who live in it.

PSALM 24:1

O GOD, our heavenly Father, you have blessed us and given us dominion over all the earth: Increase our reverence before the mystery of life; and give us new insight into your purposes for the human race, and new wisdom and determination in making provision for its future in accordance with your will. Through Jesus Christ our Lord. Amen.

—*THE BOOK OF COMMON PRAYER*

What an awesome privilege and a sobering responsibility it is to realize that today, in the choices we make, we are helping to fashion the kind of world our grandchildren will inherit and inhabit.

A glad heart makes a cheerful countenance.... A cheerful heart is a good medicine.

PROVERBS 15:13; 17:22

*G*OD, GRANT ME the ability to laugh today, if not audibly, then in my heart. Help me to lighten up and find some relief in humor when things get too intense. Show me how to be sensitive to others and to gently lead them in the direction of a smile. Come, cheer my heart right now with your own witty perspective on my life. Indeed, I can't add an inch to my height or a minute to my existence by worrying, no matter how hard I grit my teeth and clench my fists. God, I'm chuckling now, and I'm ready to face my world.

Of all days, the day on which one has not laughed is the one most surely wasted.
—SÉBASTIEN-ROCH NICOLAS DE CHAMFORT

February 20

Fight the good fight of the faith.
1 TIMOTHY 6:12

O MY FATHER, Great Elder,
I have no words to thank you,
But with your deep wisdom
I am sure that you can see
How I value your glorious gifts.
O my Father, when I look upon your greatness,
I am confounded with awe,
O Great Elder,
Ruler of all things earthly and heavenly,
I am your warrior,
Ready to act in accordance with your will.

—KIKUYU

**Administering the healing power of love to
defeat the destructive power of hatred;
wielding the freedom of truth to do battle
against the bondage of lies; ambushing the fear
of death with the hope of life. As the fight of
faith goes on all around us, may we find
ourselves fighting for love, truth, and life.**

Well meant are the wounds a friend inflicts.

PROVERBS 27:6

*L*ORD, HELP ME to be willing to receive constructive criticism from friends whom I know are looking out for my best interest. Even when I feel protests rising up inside of me, help me to hear them out and to receive their words with grace, giving careful consideration to what has been said before responding. If they have mis-understood me in some way, help me not to take offense. If we simply cannot agree, preserve our friendship with the love you have given us for each other.

A true friend loves you enough to support you and to confront you.

—ANONYMOUS

February 22

*The Lord God took the man and put him
in the garden of Eden to till it and keep it.*
GENESIS 2:15

ALMIGHTY GOD, ... you made us fellow workers in your creation; Give us wisdom and reverence so to use the resources of nature, that no one may suffer from our abuse of them, and that generations yet to come may continue to praise you for your bounty.

—*THE BOOK OF COMMON PRAYER*

A portion of the world's resources has been entrusted to me. As a good steward, what can I do today to conserve, preserve, protect, and tend my garden of responsibility? I can put those resources into concrete action.

February 23

When you are disturbed, do not sin;
ponder it on your beds and be silent.

PSALM 4:4

*W*HEN I HEAR of some of the things people are saying about me, heavenly Father, I want so much to set the record straight! I realize that I have two alternatives: To identify and confront the source, or to let it go and let the truth become self-evident. Please show me what the wisest course of action would be at this point. Then help me to follow through with confidence, knowing that you are ultimately in control of the situation. Amen.

Do not worry about others' opinions of you. Be humble and do not let yourselves ever be disturbed.

—MOTHER TERESA, *HEART OF JOY*

February 24

He raises up the poor from the dust; he lifts the needy from the ash heap.... He will guard the feet of his faithful ones.
1 SAMUEL 2:8–9

$\mathcal{W}$HEN I'M FEELING down, Lord, brought low by people or circumstances or both, lift my eyes to see your smile, lift my voice to speak your name, and lift my heart to sense your love. There's no one else who knows me as you do. There's nothing that can fill the emptiness in my soul. You are my comfort and my hope.

He that is down, needs fear no fall,
He that is low, no pride:
He that is humble, ever shall
Have God to be his guide.
—JOHN BUNYAN, *THE PILGRIM'S PROGRESS*

Do not let your hearts be troubled. Believe in God, believe also in me. In my Father's house there are many dwelling places. If it were not so, would I have told you that I go to prepare a place for you? And if I go and prepare a place for you, I will come again and will take you to myself, so that where I am, there you may be also.

JOHN 14:1–3

KNOWING THAT YOU are my true home gives me comfort in a world where there are no guarantees and where nothing is permanent. No matter where I am physically, mentally, emotionally, or spiritually, Lord, I can always return to you and feel welcomed and wanted. If it weren't for you, there would be times when I would feel homeless. Thank you for being my dwelling place forever.

Faith is the radical trust that home has always been there and always will be there.
—HENRI NOUWEN

February 26

Praise him, sun and moon;... Let them praise the name of the Lord, for he commanded and they were created.

PSALM 148:3, 5

CREATOR GOD, I especially want to thank you for two spectacular times of day: sunrise and sunset. When I'm present at one of these events, I'm drawn into silence, and yet my heart beats faster with the wonder and glory of what I see. The light that spreads across the earth and illumines the sky causes me to long for the light of your presence. Be always near me, I pray, dear Lord. Amen.

Every sunset which I witness inspires me with the desire to go to a West as distant and as fair as that into which the sun goes down.

—HENRY DAVID THOREAU, *WALKING*

For thus said the Lord God: "...In quietness and in trust shall be your strength."

ISAIAH 30:15

OUR FATHER,...We would find thee now in the privacy of our hearts, in the quiet of this moment. We would know, our Father, that thou art near us and beside us; that thou dost love us and art interested in all that we do, art concerned about all our affairs.

May we become aware of thy companionship, of him who walks beside us....

May we be convinced that even before we reach up to thee, thou art reaching down to us.

—PETER MARSHALL

Although we are often conversing, we can learn to value the moments when our souls commune on a level beyond words in our most intimate relationships, especially in our relationship with God.

February 28

How very good and pleasant it is when kindred live together in unity!

*F*OR THE JOY of human love,
Brother, sister, parent, child;
Friends on earth and friends above;
For all gentle thoughts and mild;
Lord of all, to Thee we raise
This our hymn of grateful praise.

—FOLLIOTT S. PIERPOINT, *FOR THE BEAUTY OF THE EARTH*

When was the last time you saw a family enjoying one another's company? Maybe it was at your own family's last gathering. Or maybe it was the last time you watched an episode of *The Waltons*. Whenever, wherever it was, think about how seeing those family ties made you feel. This is the unity for which we long in our relationships with friends and family, and working toward it is always a worthy pursuit.

Do not be conformed to this world, but be transformed by the renewing of your minds, so that you may discern what is the will of God—what is good and acceptable and perfect.

ROMANS 12:2

GOD OUR FATHER, you see your children growing up in an unsteady and confusing world: Show them that your ways give more life than the ways of the world, and that following you is better than chasing after selfish goals. Help them to take failure, not as a measure of their worth, but as a chance for a new start. Give them strength to hold their faith in you, and to keep alive their joy in your creation.

—*THE BOOK OF COMMON PRAYER*

It takes a strong fish to swim upstream. Flex your fins today, and go against the flow!

🐚 *My prayer life:*

_____

_____

_____

_____

_____

_____

_____

_____

_____

_____

_____

_____

_____

_____

March 1

*If I take the wings of the morning and
settle at the farthest limits of the sea, even
there your hand shall lead me, and your
right hand shall hold me fast.*

PSALM 139:9–10

*H*EAVENLY FATHER, my life is full of adventure. It gives
me a sense of anticipation and excitement, especially
now when I am beginning a new month. What is
unknown to me is not frightening when you are with
me. And because I know you're here, I don't mind taking
the kinds of risks that help me grow in my faith. Lead me
today even more into the adventure of living.

**There are no signposts in the sky to show a
man has passed that way before. There are no
channels marked. The flier breaks each second
into new uncharted seas.**

—ANNE MORROW LINDBERGH, *NORTH TO THE ORIENT*

March 2

The one who sows bountifully will also reap bountifully.... You will be enriched in every way for your great generosity.
2 CORINTHIANS 9:6, 11

ALMIGHTY GOD, whose loving hand hath given us all that we possess: Grant us grace that we may honor thee with our substance, and, remembering the account which we must one day give, may we be faithful stewards of thy bounty, through Jesus Christ our Lord. Amen.
—THE BOOK OF COMMON PRAYER

We can give much and still have given little. By the same token, we can give little and have given all. It is not the amount we give that determines our generosity but the depth of our giving relative to our resources. Sometimes the smallest gifts have come from the most generous hearts.

March 3

Esau ran to meet [his estranged brother, Jacob], and embraced him, and fell on his neck and kissed him, and they wept.

GENESIS 33:4

LORD, I want to lay down the boxing gloves today and leave the fighting behind us. It's time to stop, to forgive, and to heal. Show me how to reconcile and how to be humble without being a doormat. I want us both to walk away with our respect for one another intact, and I'm hopeful that beyond the mutual respect there will be a deepening love.

March 4

*May God be gracious to us and bless us
and make his face to shine upon us, that
your way may be known upon the earth,
your saving power among all nations.*

PSALM 67:1–2

BLESS TO ME, O God, the earth beneath my feet,
Bless to me, O God, the path whereon I go,
Bless to me, O God, the people whom I meet,
Today, tonight and tomorrow. Amen.

—ANCIENT CELTIC PRAYER

**Every person with whom I interact today will
be affected to some degree by me. I may be able
to persuade them, however slightly or signifi-
cantly, to be kinder, happier, and more serene.
And if I happen to succeed in tipping the scales
in the right direction, then I have made a positive difference in the world.**

This one thing I do: forgetting what lies behind and straining forward to what lies ahead, I press on toward the goal for the prize of the heavenly call of God.

PHILIPPIANS 3:13–14

I USED TO BELIEVE that the failures of yesterday would haunt me forever, Lord. But in your mercy, you have given me the gift of a wonderful today and a hopeful tomorrow. Thank you for second chances, for clean slates, for new opportunities, and for lessons learned. When I see others who suffer from the pain of the past, let me be a minister of mercy, encouraging them to leave behind their mistakes and to walk with peace and confidence toward the future.

We have to do with the past only as we can make it useful to the present and the future.

—FREDERICK DOUGLASS

March 6

Happy are those who fear the Lord, who greatly delight in his commandments.... they are gracious, merciful, and righteous.... They are not afraid of evil tidings; their hearts are firm, secure in the Lord. Their hearts are steady, they will not be afraid; in the end they will look in triumph on their foes.

PSALM 112:1, 4, 7–8

*D*EAR GOD, the courage I have today to stand up for what is right comes from my confidence that you stand behind me. Wherever there is oppression, injustice, and evil, I know that you oppose such tyranny, and so must I. Be with me now as I proclaim your justice, and help me to be merciful as well. Amen.

Jesus said, "Let the little children come to me, and do not stop them; for it is to such as these that the kingdom of heaven belongs."

MATTHEW 19:14

*H*EAVENLY FATHER, who has put within the hearts of children the kind of pure faith that is fit for heaven, remind us how to have that kind of trust in you. Help us to humble ourselves and to put aside our foolish thoughts of self-sufficiency and self-importance. Teach us to lay down our fears and anxieties and to allow you to carry us in times of trouble and comfort us in times of sadness. Forgive our prideful denial of our need for you. We long to inhabit your kingdom with you, living forever as your children.

Blessed be childhood, which brings down something of heaven into the midst of our rough earthliness.

—HENRI FREDERIC AMIEL

March 8

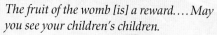

The fruit of the womb [is] a reward....May
you see your children's children.

PSALMS 127:3; 128:6

THE CHILDREN YOU'VE placed in
my life, heavenly Father, remind
me that life is for living. Their
unique personalities remind me
that you've made each of your
children special. Their energy
fosters joy, and I long for the
kind of trust they have. Keep the
children near me, Lord; always
let my heart be taken by them.
For by these little ones, I am
reminded how to live.

Jesus said, "All things can be done for the one who believes."
MARK 9:23

You ARE GOD, whose imagination brought into existence an amazing array of plants and animals, the remarkable depths of skies and seas, and the grandeur of stars and mountains. You made the mind and spirit of humankind, and you stamped on each of us your own image. O Creator God, whose dreams are brought to life by your will, grant me courage to dream and the faith to believe that you can cause my dreams to live. Amen.

March 10

The Lord is my shepherd.... He maketh me to lie down in green pastures: he leadeth me beside the still waters. He restoreth my soul: he leadeth me in the paths of righteousness for his name's sake.

PSALM 23:1–3, KJV

SAVIOUR, like a shepherd, lead us,
Much we need Thy tenderest care;
In Thy pleasant pastures feed us,
For our use Thy folds prepare.

We are Thine; do Thou befriend us,
Be the guardian of our way;
Keep Thy flock, from sin defend us,
Seek us if we go astray.
—ATTRIBUTED TO DOROTHY A. THRUPP

Jesus is not a crutch; he's our shepherd. Crutches merely prop us up when we are hurting; Jesus offers healing, nourishment, guidance, and a safe place for us to grow strong.

Have nothing to do with stupid and senseless controversies; you know that they breed quarrels. And the Lord's servant must not be quarrelsome but kindly to everyone, an apt teacher, patient, correcting opponents with gentleness.

2 TIMOTHY 2:23–25

WHEN I AM TEMPTED to engage in a heated argument, Lord, please give me the wisdom and strength I need to keep my cool and to maintain a productive discussion. I want to be the kind of person who is able to have a disagreement without thinking of my opponent as the enemy. I also need your insight for knowing which issues are worth fighting for and which ones I should let go. This is touchy business, God, and I admit that I don't always succeed in doing it right. But I want to improve. Please help me.

If you would win a man to your cause, first convince him that you are his sincere friend. Therein is a drop of honey that catches his heart, which, say what you will, is the great high-road to his reason, and which, when once gained, you will find but little trouble in convincing his judgment of the justice of your cause.

—ABRAHAM LINCOLN

March 12

Bless the Lord, O my soul, and do not forget all his benefits—
who forgives all your iniquity, who heals all your diseases, who
redeems your life from the Pit, who crowns you with steadfast
love and mercy, who satisfies you with good as long as you live
so that your youth is renewed like the eagle's.

PSALM 103:2–5

HEAL US, LORD, and we shall
be healed; save us and we shall
be saved; for it is You we praise.
Send relief and healing for all our
diseases, our sufferings and our
wounds; for You are a merciful
and faithful healer. Blessed are
You, Lord, who heals the sick.
—TRADITIONAL JEWISH PRAYER

When our longing to be healed–mind, soul, or body–seems
unnoticed by God, remember that his love for us is complete, his
purpose for us is good, and his timing for us is perfect. We will
be healed–to one degree or another on this side of heaven, but
ultimately and entirely on the other side.

March 13

Thus you shall say to my servant David: Thus says the Lord of hosts: I took you from the pasture, from following the sheep to be prince over my people Israel; … and I will make for you a great name, like the name of the great ones of the earth.

2 SAMUEL 7:8–9

Yours, O LORD, are the greatness, the power, the glory, the victory, and the majesty; for all that is in the heavens and on the earth is yours; yours is the kingdom, O Lord, and you are exalted as head above all. Riches and honor come from you, and you rule over all. In your hand are power and might; and it is in your hand to make great and to give strength to all. And now, our God, we give thanks to you and praise your glorious name.

—KING DAVID OF ISRAEL (1 CHRONICLES 29:11–13)

God sometimes grants us greatness for the purpose of demonstrating how great and good he is so that others may come to know him and experience his love.

March 14

All must test their own work; then that work, rather than their neighbor's work, will become a cause for pride. For all must carry their own loads.

GALATIANS 6:4–5

You call me to be a responsible person, Lord, to work hard with the strength you have given me, to take pride in what I do so that the excellence in my work will reflect your excellence, and to be honest with myself about how I'm doing. I receive your grace today, God. As I live in that grace, be pleased with my efforts to be a responsible person.

I don't know who my grandfather was; I am much more concerned to know what his grandson will be.

—ABRAHAM LINCOLN

March 15

Some friends play at friendship but a true friend sticks closer than one's nearest kin.

PROVERBS 18:24

I SHOOK HANDS with my friend, Lord,
And suddenly when I saw his sad and anxious face,
I feared that you were not in his heart.
I am troubled as I am before a closed tabernacle when
    there is no light to show that you are there.
If you were not there, Lord, my friend and I would be
    separated.
For his hand in mine would be only flesh in flesh
And his love for me that of man for man.
I want your life for him as well as for me.
For it is only in you that he can be my brother.

—MICHEL QUOIST, "MY FRIEND," *PRAYERS OF LIFE*

It is only when God breathes life into a friendship that it becomes an exquisite joy that will live for an eternity.

March 16

As long as the earth endures, seedtime and harvest, cold and heat, summer and winter, day and night, shall not cease.

GENESIS 8:22

CREATOR GOD, winter is moving toward spring, and I welcome the change. Thank you for the gift of variety in your design. Thank you for the joys of anticipation, for the certainty of hope, and for the expectation this gradual transition brings. Winter to spring, cold to warm, shorter days to longer ones. It's a wonder to behold. Your works are amazing indeed!

It was one of those March days when the sun shines hot and the wind blows cold; when it is summer in the light, and winter in the shade.

—CHARLES DICKENS, *GREAT EXPECTATIONS*

March 17

*The Lord looks down from heaven
on humankind to see if there are any
who are wise, who seek after God.*

PSALM 14:2

BE THOU MY vision, O Lord of my heart;
Naught be all else to me, save that thou art,
Thou my best thought, by day or by night,
Waking or sleeping, thy presence my light.

—TRADITIONAL IRISH PRAYER

**Because God is good, he loves to bless us,
but his deepest longing is for a relationship with us. Today as we enjoy the good
things our heavenly Father has given us,
may we take some time to commune
with him, to grow closer to him, and to
get to know him a little better.**

March 18

Unless the Lord builds the house,
those who build it labor in vain.

PSALM 127:1

LORD, you are the foundation of my life. When circumstances shift and make my world unsteady, you remain firm. When threats of what lies ahead blow against the framework of my thoughts, you are solid. When I focus on your steadfastness, I realize that you are my strength for the moment, the one sure thing in my life. Because of you I stand now, and I will stand tomorrow as well because you are there already. Amen.

Stay focused on how to best serve the present by keeping your foundation strong, and the future ultimately will prosper.

—VIVIAN ELISABETH GLYCK, *LIFE I LEARNED FROM MY GARDEN*

One who spares words is knowledgeable; one who is cool in spirit has understanding. Even fools who keep silent are considered wise; when they close their lips, they are deemed intelligent.

PROVERBS 17:27–28

WHEN I CONSIDER how much talking I do in your presence, Lord God, I realize that you are the consummate listener. How comforted I am to know you are listening to me—hearing my every word and sensing my every concern, need, and joy. Now teach me the art of listening so that I can listen to you and others. Help me be a good listener like you.

March 20

Search me, O God, and know my heart;
test me and know my thoughts. See if
there is any wicked way in me, and lead
me in the way everlasting.

PSALM 139:23–24

$\mathcal{H}$EAVENLY FATHER, so often my pride stands in the way of real peace and happiness, not only peace and happiness for myself, but also for those around me. And the truth is, I need your help to conquer this self-serving nature of mine, because I see how deep it runs and I know from experience that it's beyond my control. Please teach me to let go of my stubborn insistence that things go my way. Loosen my death grip on the need to be first and best. Forgive me for trying so hard to control what others think and do. Show me how to embrace humility without resentment. I know this will be a process, God, so help me to hang in there as we go through it together.

How can we overcome this deadly virus called pride? . . . You start by taking a long look within. What do you see? What do others see inside of us? Who is that person mirrored in your soul? It takes guts to do this!

—ROBERT STRAND, *A LITTLE TOUCH OF HEAVEN*

Those who despise their neighbors are sinners,
but happy are those who are kind to the poor.
PROVERBS 14:21

DEAR HEAVENLY FATHER,
today, if I see or hear of someone who is struggling in some
way, please help me take a
moment to remember what it
was like when I was struggling
and you helped me through the
aid of a friend or a stranger. Let
that memory mobilize me to
offer help and be your true
servant. This I pray. Amen.

March 22

As an eagle stirs up its nest, and hovers over its young; as it spreads its wings, takes them up, and bears them aloft on its pinions, the Lord alone guided [Jacob].... He set him atop the heights of the land.

DEUTERONOMY 32:11–13

WHEN CHANGE COMES, Lord, I'm not always prepared to view it in a positive light, but help me to not dwell on my fears and on all the things that could go wrong. Instead, show me what positive things might result from this new development. Then, as I focus on the good, you will turn my fears into faith—faith that you are carrying me along, teaching me to trust, helping me to grow stronger, and showing me a new part of your plan for my life. Give me courage to embrace the adventure and trust that you are leading me toward something wonderful.

For this perishable body must put on imperishability, and this mortal body must put on immortality.

1 CORINTHIANS 15:53

LORD OF THE RESURRECTION, I cannot begin to comprehend what it means to, one day, be clothed with the imperishable, to put on immortality as if it were a garment. But I want to prepare for that glorious day as I demonstrate compassion, kindness, humility, gentleness, and patience to all those around me. Prepare me for heaven. Fit me for eternity. Fashion me into the person You want me to be so that I will be ready for my eternal clothes of righteousness.

—JONI EARECKSON TADA, *DIAMONDS IN THE DUST*

Resurrection is new life. It is our promise from God and our hope for the future. We live today as people with a purpose because we believe there is an eternity for which God is preparing us.

● *March 24*

*But it is for you, O Lord, that I wait; it is
you, O Lord my God, who will answer.*
PSALM 38:15

SOMETIMES MY HEART is so overwhelmed,
God, that I don't know where to begin my
prayer. Help me to quiet my soul and remember that you know everything inside of my
mind before I ever come to you with it. But
still, I need to tell you about it, Lord, and I
know you have said that you want me to tell
you. Thank you for being such a faithful
listener and for caring about everything that
concerns me. When I remember that, it helps
me slow down, take a deep breath, and
finally begin the conversation. OK. I'm ready
now to talk…and to listen.

March 25

*A generous person will be enriched, and
one who gives water will get water.*

Proverbs 11:25

*L*ORD, HELP ME not be a taker but a tender,
Lord, help me not be a whiner but a worker,
Lord, help me not be a getter but a giver,
Lord, help me not be a hindrance but a help,
Lord, help me not be a critic but a catalyst for good.

—MARIAN WRIGHT EDELMAN, *GUIDE MY FEET*

**When we turn our focus away from our own
apparent neediness and, instead, turn our energies
toward helping others in need, we are surprisingly
enriched, and often we discover that we are not
really as needy as we once thought we were.**

March 26

*Be subject to one another out of reverence for Christ.
…Each of you…should love his wife as himself, and a
wife should respect her husband. Children, obey your
parents in the Lord, for this is right.*

EPHESIANS 5:21, 33—6:1

*H*EAVENLY FATHER, who serves your children with love
and abandon—blessing, nurturing, saving, healing, and
transforming us—please teach me your style of serving.
When I feel taxed by my family, remind me to come to
you and find restoration for my weary body and soul.
When I feel annoyed by them, help me to remember how
important they are to me and how I would feel if I did
not have them in my life anymore. When I am tempted
to give up on them, give me a new measure of faith and
hope for them. As you are to me, let me be to them.

**Family. It has a dozen definitions,
but it's taken from the Latin word
famulus meaning "servant."**
—JANE KIRKPATRICK, *A BURDEN SHARED*

The boundary lines have fallen for me in pleasant places; I have a goodly heritage.... I keep the Lord always before me; because he is at my right hand, I shall not be moved. Therefore... my body also rests secure.

PSALM 16:6, 8–9

LORD I'VE PUT my trust in thee,
  And I'm content;
Whatsoe'er my lot may be,
'Though my way I may not see;
  And I'm content.

Lord I feel thy Presence near,
  And I'm content.
In thy care, I know not fear,
'Though the Tempter's voice I hear;
I'm secure when Thou art near;
  And I'm content.

—PRISCILLA JANE THOMPSON

As I take inventory of the benefits I enjoy today, discontent gets pushed away and a renewed sense of gratitude and joy rises up within me.

March 28

But be doers of the word, and not merely hearers who deceive themselves.

JAMES 1:22

𝓗EAVENLY FATHER, I'm aware that there is an area of my life that you want me to deal with. I feel like hiding from this challenge, but I know that it's not going away. Please direct me to the sources of help that you have prepared for me. Help me to overcome my fear and pride in order to move forward. Grant me courage and determination until I have gained the victory.

Happy are those who do not follow the advice of the wicked, or take the path that sinners tread, or sit in the seat of scoffers; but their delight is in the law of the Lord, and on his law they meditate day and night.

PSALM 1:1–2

*D*EAR LORD, if I am to succeed meaningfully in this life, I must succeed first in being a person rich in integrity and love. Only then will all other successes find their significance. I know this is true because you've told me this so many times in the past. Please continue to help me be the person you want me to be. Amen.

March 30

*Now faith is the assurance of things hoped
for, the conviction of things not seen.*

HEBREWS 11:1

GOD OF MY LIFE, though you are not visible to me, I see
evidence of your existence everywhere I look. Though I
cannot reach out and touch your face, I sense your presence with me. You speak to me in silent ways with an
inaudible voice. How can I explain this mystery—what
I know to be true but cannot prove? This spiritual
sensitivity—this awareness of you—is more real to me
than the pages on which my eyes fall at this moment.
You exist, and I believe.

**I believe in the sun even when it does not shine
I believe in love even when I do not feel it
I believe in God even when He is silent.**

—AUTHOR UNKNOWN (INSCRIBED ON A CELLAR WALL IN COLOGNE,
GERMANY, WHERE JEWS HID FROM NAZI SOLDIERS)

March 31 🐚

God saw everything that he had made,
and indeed, it was very good.

GENESIS 1:31

$\mathcal{M}$Y DEAR LORD, as I enjoy the beauty
of nature, I can remember that when you
created the world, you took time to step
back and enjoy what you had made. In like
manner, it is good for me to pause from
time to time and delight in the work of my
hands. Thank you that I can say what I
make is good, because your hands were on
mine. This I pray. Amen.

My prayer life:

_____

_____

_____

_____

_____

_____

_____

_____

_____

_____

_____

_____

_____

April 1

*Honor the Lord with your substance and
with the first fruits of all your produce;
then your barns will be filled with plenty,
and your vats will be bursting with wine.*

PROVERBS 3:9–10

GIVER OF ALL good gifts, thank you for providing
what I need today. As I enjoy the abundance in my life,
stir my heart with compassion for those—both nearby
and far away—who struggle to find a way to survive—
spiritually, emotionally, and physically. And as I look
for opportunities to share the resources I have, grant
me special wisdom to know how and to whom I
should give. Finally, I ask that you bless and multiply
these tokens of my gratitude. May praise come to you
through the charity you inspire in my heart. Amen.

**I deem it the duty of every man to devote a certain
portion of his income for charitable purposes; and
that is his further duty to see it so applied as to do
the most good to which it is capable.**

—THOMAS JEFFERSON

April 2

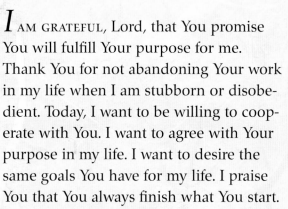

Trust in the Lord with all your heart, and do not rely on your own insight. In all your ways acknowledge him, and he will make straight your paths.

PROVERBS 3:5–6

I AM GRATEFUL, Lord, that You promise You will fulfill Your purpose for me. Thank You for not abandoning Your work in my life when I am stubborn or disobedient. Today, I want to be willing to cooperate with You. I want to agree with Your purpose in my life. I want to desire the same goals You have for my life. I praise You that You always finish what You start.

—JONI EARECKSON TADA, *DIAMONDS IN THE DUST*

When I think I see clearly, I may be wrong. Only God has the vantage point of eternity, and only he knows for sure which way I should go from here.

> *Jesus told them many things in parables, saying, "Listen!*
> *A sower went out to sow. And as he sowed, some ... seeds*
> *fell among thorns, and the thorns grew up and choked*
> *them. ... this is the one who hears the word, but the cares*
> *of the world and the lure of wealth choke the word, and it*
> *yields nothing."*
>
> MATTHEW 13:3–4, 7, 22

LORD, sometimes my life feels out of control. Too many things are going on, and there's no time to do anything I enjoy. When that happens, I feel as if I lose touch with you and with the part of myself that knows how to laugh and be lighthearted. My schedule becomes a list of demands that brings pressure, stress, and anxiety. Please show me how to break free by pruning back my activities and weeding out those demands that cause needless stress. And as you show me what to do, help me have the determination and the courage to follow through and make changes. Lead me to laughter and joy again, I pray.

As hard as it is, when life starts growing wildly in every direction, get out those shears and skillfully snip away the excess that robs your spirit of essential growth.
—VIVIAN ELISABETH GLYCK, *LIFE I LEARNED FROM MY GARDEN*

April 4

As [Jesus] was walking along, he saw Levi son of Alphaeus sitting at the tax booth, and he said to him, "Follow me." And he got up and followed him.

MARK 2:14

$\mathcal{D}$EAR HOLY FATHER, I admit quite often during the day the furthest thing from my mind is thinking about how I can follow the path of your Son and how I can best please you. Remind me every moment through your Spirit that I am yours and that I can be content only when I obey you in all that I do. Amen.

When you concern yourself only with Jesus' opinion of you, life suddenly becomes far less complicated, emptied of fears and regrets, and filled up with honesty and love.

But speaking the truth in love, we must grow up in every way into him who is the head, into Christ.

EPHESIANS 4:15

LORD GOD, when I'm tempted today to amend the truth about something to preserve my image, help me to remember that lies compound themselves and are far more difficult to face later on than the truth is right now. So instead of my trying to alter some account of what has happened, help me to work on changing my attitudes, behaviors, and words so that I won't feel the need to hide behind a lie.

No man has enough memory to be a successful liar.

—ABRAHAM LINCOLN

April 6

I will look with favor on the faithful in the land, so that they may live with me; whoever walks in the way that is blameless shall minister to me.

PSALM 101:6

O FILL ME with Thy fulness, Lord
Until my very heart o'erflow
In kindling thought and glowing word,
Thy love to tell, Thy praise to show.

O use me, Lord, use even me
Just as Thou wilt, and when, and where;
Until Thy blessed face I see,
Thy rest, Thy joy, Thy glory share. Amen.

—FRANCES R. HAVERGAL

Today there will be many opportunities to do good; if I choose to act on even one of those opportunities, I will have introduced a new bit of blessing into the world.

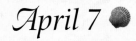

*I press on toward the goal for the prize of
the heavenly call of God in Christ Jesus.*
PHILIPPIANS 3:14

JESUS, YOU CAME into the world, grew up in
an ordinary family, lived in an ordinary vil-
lage, and were trained to be an ordinary
carpenter. However, your life was in no way
ordinary. In courage, you embraced your
heavenly Father's plan. In faith-filled obedience, you saw it through. In glory, you now
live, inspiring those who follow your example. Help me be a disciple whose life is made
extraordinary by your presence in it.

April 8

Of making many books there is no end, and much study is a weariness of the flesh....Fear God, and keep his commandments; for that is the whole duty of everyone.

ECCLESIASTES 12:12–13

O GOD, who art the truth, make me one with Thee in continual love! I am weary often to read and hear many things. In Thee is all that I desire and long for. Let all teachers hold their peace; let all creatures be silent in Thy sight; speak to me alone.

—THOMAS Á KEMPIS,
THE IMITATION OF CHRIST

When confusion sets in, and when there is too much advice coming from too many places, don't forget God, his wisdom, and his Word.

The Lord does not see as mortals see; they look on the outward appearance, but the Lord looks on the heart.

1 SAMUEL 16:7

*L*ORD, despite my best efforts, I sometimes fall short of my goals. Help me not get discouraged and stop trying, especially when others become disappointed in me. Instead, remind me that you care about who I am rather than what I have achieved. Thank you for seeing the longings and desires that lie behind my struggles.

Men judge us by the success of our efforts. God looks at the efforts themselves.

—CHARLOTTE BRONTË

Know that the Lord is God. It is he that made us, and we are his; we are his people, and the sheep of his pasture.

PSALM 100:3

*L*ORD, WE PRAY for unity and harmony in the world. Help us to be a positive force for bringing all your children together in love and peace.

Today I visited a rose garden in which flowers bloomed in an array of colors. Each separate flower was exquisite and lovely, while each variety of rose was set off in its special uniqueness by the different ones around it. How very much like our garden of humanity! As we bloom side by side, may we rejoice not only in our own beauty but also in the unique beauty of those whom God has planted here with us.

April 11

God did not give us a spirit of cowardice, but rather a spirit of power and of love and of self-discipline.

2 TIMOTHY 1:7

$\mathcal{H}$EAVENLY FATHER, it's both exciting and scary as I consider forging ahead and taking a risk. I don't want to act rashly and then regret my decision. But I also don't want to let my fear control the choices I make. Help me choose wisely and step carefully so that I move forward in a positive direction. Thank you for your guiding presence and for your unconditional love that gives me the courage to take action.

Risk taking is definitely risky, but you never have to "risk everything." You just have to risk wisely.
—CHARLIE HEDGES, *GETTING THE RIGHT THINGS RIGHT*

April 12

All this is from God, who reconciled us to himself through Christ, and has given us the ministry of reconciliation; that is, in Christ God was reconciling the world to himself, not counting their trespasses against them, and entrusting the message of reconciliation to us.

2 CORINTHIANS 5:18–19

O GOD, the Father of all, whose Son commanded us to love our enemies: Lead them and us from prejudice to truth; deliver them and us from hatred, cruelty, and revenge; and in your good time enable us all to stand reconciled before you; through Jesus Christ our Lord. Amen.

—*THE BOOK OF COMMON PRAYER*

Forgiveness opens the door to reconciliation. When we open that door, others may choose not to walk through it. But regardless of their decision, we ourselves remain free from the burden of hatred.

April 13

*For it is the God who said, "Let light
shine out of darkness," who has shone in
our hearts…We are afflicted in every
way, but not crushed; perplexed, but not
driven to despair; persecuted, but not
forsaken; struck down, but not destroyed.*

2 CORINTHIANS 4:6, 8–9

LORD, SOMETIMES the weight of circumstances feels too heavy for me, but I know
that you promised not to give me more
than I can bear. So today as you give me
strength to live, help me not carry the
unnecessary concerns of tomorrow. Show
me the light of your truth and the promise
of your goodness as I learn to trust you.

**Sometimes God sends the brilliant light of a rainbow to remind
us of his presence, lest we forget in our personal darkness his
great and gracious promises to never leave us alone.**

—VERDELL DAVIS, *RICHES STORED IN SECRET PLACES*

April 14

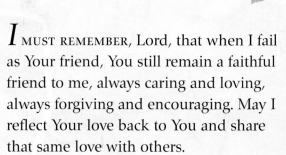

If we are faithless, he remains faithful—
for he cannot deny himself.

2 TIMOTHY 2:13

I MUST REMEMBER, Lord, that when I fail as Your friend, You still remain a faithful friend to me, always caring and loving, always forgiving and encouraging. May I reflect Your love back to You and share that same love with others.

—JONI EARECKSON TADA, *DIAMONDS IN THE DUST*

God is the eternally vigilant and perfect friend. When we are out of line, he tells us the truth without malice. When we are hurting, he soothes us with his pure, selfless love. And though we fail him from time to time, his love is never withdrawn from us.

April 15

For you were called to freedom, brothers and sisters; only do not use your freedom as an opportunity for self-indulgence, ... the fruit of the Spirit is love, joy, peace, patience, kindness, generosity, faithfulness, gentleness, and self-control.

GALATIANS 5:13, 22–23

I FEEL FREE in your love, God. I feel as if I can live free from others' opinions, free from guilt, and free from fear because no matter what, your love is there for me. But I know that freedom can be abused, so help me remember that I also have been freed from the tyranny of fear, hatred, and arrogance. Help me exercise self-discipline so that I do not enslave myself to foolish extremes you never intended for me. Show me how to remain free and to lead others into your sanctuary of peace and freedom. Amen.

Some people regard discipline as a chore. For me, it is a kind of order that sets me free to fly.

—JULIE ANDREWS

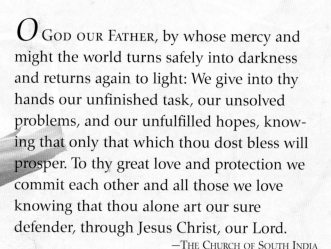

April 16

I waited patiently for the Lord; he inclined to me and heard my cry. He drew me up from the desolate pit, out of the miry bog, and set my feet upon a rock, making my steps secure.

PSALM 40:1–2

O GOD OUR FATHER, by whose mercy and might the world turns safely into darkness and returns again to light: We give into thy hands our unfinished task, our unsolved problems, and our unfulfilled hopes, knowing that only that which thou dost bless will prosper. To thy great love and protection we commit each other and all those we love knowing that thou alone art our sure defender, through Jesus Christ, our Lord.

—THE CHURCH OF SOUTH INDIA

God is in our past; he has brought us through it. God is in our present; he is walking beside us even now. God is in our future; he will lead us safely there.

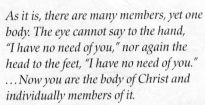

April 17

As it is, there are many members, yet one body. The eye cannot say to the hand, "I have no need of you," nor again the head to the feet, "I have no need of you." …Now you are the body of Christ and individually members of it.

1 CORINTHIANS 12:20–21, 27

SOMETIMES, LORD, I wonder where I fit in and where I belong. I feel as if I don't have a clear purpose and that my life is insignificant. But you created me, and you know for what purpose and to what end I was made. Please open my eyes to your plan, to the uniqueness of my life, and to the purpose of my existence. As I discover who you created me to be and what you created me to do, help me find fresh joy and a renewed energy for life. Thank you for giving me meaning. Amen.

Every human being has some handle by which he may be lifted, some groove in which he was meant to run; and the great work of life, as far as our relations with each other are concerned, is to lift each one by his own proper handle, and run each one in his own proper groove.

—HARRIET BEECHER STOWE, *LITTLE FOXES*

April 18

I delight to do your will, O my God;
your law is within my heart.

PSALM 40:8

TAKE MY LIFE, and let it be
Consecrated, Lord, to Thee.
Take my moments and my days,
Let them flow in ceaseless praise.
Let them flow in ceaseless praise.

Take my love; my Lord, I pour
At Thy feet its treasure store.
Take myself, and I will be
Ever, only, all for Thee,
Ever, only, all for Thee.

—FRANCES R. HAVERGAL

People are never more happy or fulfilled than when they are moving within the loving will of their Designer.

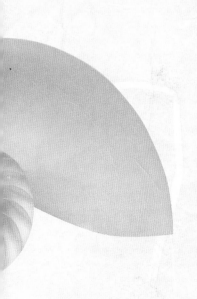

May the Lord give you increase, both you and your children. May you be blessed by the Lord, who made heaven and earth.

PSALM 115:14–15

*H*EAVENLY FATHER, I see possibilities of what could be a better future. I want to make a real difference in my world, but sometimes I get bogged down by obstacles, complacency, and discouragement. Lift me up again, dear God. Give me your vision, your strength, your plan, your inspiration, and your love so I may be a positive force for those who come after me.

An idealist is a person who helps other people to be prosperous.

—HENRY FORD

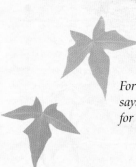 *April 20*

For surely I know the plans I have for you,
says the Lord, plans for your welfare and not
for harm, to give you a future with hope.

JEREMIAH 29:11

FATHER, I trust You. I know that Your plans
are for good and not for harm. I know that
You know the whole picture and are acting in
accordance with it. I know that You only tear
down in order to build up. I know that You
only empty in order to fill. Let Your will be
done. In Jesus' Name.

—JENNIFER KENNEDY DEAN, *POWER PRAYING*

Even though you feel as if you
can't possibly be on the right
path, keep following God. He
knows the way home.

Blessed are the poor in spirit, for theirs is the kingdom of heaven.
MATTHEW 5:3

GOD, when I am honest with you about myself, I'm afraid that you won't love me, because there are these undesirable parts within me—the broken parts, the ugly parts, the proud parts, and the selfish parts—that I fear will bring your rejection. But I'm tired of hiding from you. You already see inside of me, and you see all of me, and still you love me. Please help me to let go of my self-deception and to stop trying to maintain a false image. I long to rest in your love instead of always trying to earn it. Amen.

Getting honest with ourselves does not make us unacceptable to God. It does not distance us from God, but draws us to him—as nothing else can—and opens us anew to the flow of grace.

—BRENNAN MANNING

April 22

Now the winter is past, the rain is over and gone. The flowers appear on the earth; the time of singing has come, and the voice of the turtledove is heard in our land. The fig tree puts forth its figs, and the vines are in blossom; they give forth fragrance.

SONG OF SOLOMON 2:11–13

THE YEAR'S AT the spring,
And day's at the morn;
Morning's at seven;
the hill-side's dew-pearled;
the lark's on the wing;
The snail's on the thorn;
God's in His heaven—
All's right with the world!
—ROBERT BROWNING

**We can't help but step into spring
with a spring in our step!**

> *God opposes the proud, but gives grace to*
> *the humble ... Humble yourselves before*
> *the Lord, and he will exalt you.*
>
> JAMES 4:6, 10

*L*ORD, GRANT ME true humility whatever my circumstance. Teach me how to be pleased with a job I've done well without becoming puffed up with self-importance. Help me learn to receive praise with gratitude, focusing on the kindness of those who offer me their encouragement. Then, Lord, when I find I have done something foolish, help me to avoid compounding the problem with my prideful excuses, anger, or blaming. Help me take responsibility for what I've done and rest in your grace and forgiveness. Amen.

It is no great thing to be humble when you are brought low; but to be humble when you are praised is a great and rare attainment.

—ST. BERNARD OF CLAIRVAUX

April 24

*Surely goodness and mercy shall
follow me all the days of my life, and
I shall dwell in the house of the Lord
my whole life long.*

PSALM 23:6

*L*ORD, let me always say Yes to tomorrow.
—DALE EVANS ROGERS, *SAY YES TO TOMORROW*

I had planned a little outing for my two nephews. We were going to walk on a beautiful trail in the countryside, a habitat for wild bunnies, garden snakes, and birds of all kinds. There are bridges that span the streams and a snack bar at the trail's head. However, at the news that they could not bring their bicycles along, the older boy chose to stay home and sulk. The younger, more able to let go of his expectations, decided he'd take the adventure for what it would offer, minus his bicycle. He returned home with tales of snake catching and chipmunk sightings, and as he chattered excitedly, his brother's sulking gave way to visible regret. Later, as I considered their responses, I wondered, *How often do I say no to God's good plans for me because I insist that he operate on my terms?* Oh, how I want to learn more and more to be flexible, to let go of today's agenda and embrace tomorrow's wonders.

April 25 🐚

Weeping may linger for the night, but joy comes with the morning....You have ... clothed me with joy, so that my soul may praise you and not be silent.
PSALM 30:5, 11–12

$\mathcal{G}$OD, when I'm sad, I love how you sit in the silence with me, just being there with your comforting presence surrounding me and easing my sorrow. It makes it easier for me to let go of my sorrow and accept the joy that you want me to have. You never push nor chide. Thank you for your gentleness and for the hope you always hold out to me. When I am done crying, I know you will be there to help me laugh again.

God does not stifle our tears; He turns them into joy.
—JANETTE OKE, THE FAITHFUL FATHER

April 26

*My people will abide in a peaceful
habitation, in secure dwellings, and
in quiet resting places.*

ISAIAH 32:18

O GOD, make us children of quietness
and heirs of peace. Amen.

—ST. CLEMENT

**Take time to unwind, time to be silent, time to
reflect, and time to pray. Then calm will replace
anxiety, clarity will chase away confusion, and
refreshment will erase exhaustion. Schedule
these times of solitude. Make them a way of
life. Then peace will become your hallmark,
and each day God gives you will be a blessing.**

Beloved, never avenge yourselves, but leave room for the wrath of God; for it is written, "Vengeance is mine, I will repay, says the Lord."...Do not be overcome by evil, but overcome evil with good.

ROMANS 12:19, 21

WHEN OTHER PEOPLE hurt me, heavenly Father, I want so much to strike out at them and hurt them back. But I know retaliation isn't right and only makes the situation worse: The anger escalates, and nothing is solved. Help me, Lord, to do things your way and have the strength not to take revenge. Help me to trust that you will deal with the situation in your own time and in your own way—the best way. But, Lord, while I'm praying, I realize that just restraining my anger really isn't enough. Help me to move toward forgiveness, for in forgiveness I find release from bitterness and the freedom to move on in peace.

To forgive someone is to display reverence. Forgiveness is not saying the one who hurt you was right. Forgiveness is stating that God is fair and he will do what is right.

—MAX LUCADO, *WHEN GOD WHISPERS YOUR NAME*

April 28

But now thus says the Lord, he who created you, O Jacob, he who formed you, O Israel: Do not fear, for I have redeemed you; I have called you by name, you are mine. When you pass through the waters, I will be with you; and through the rivers, they shall not overwhelm you; when you walk through the fire you shall not be burned, and the flame shall not consume you. For I am the Lord your God, the Holy One of Israel, your Savior.

ISAIAH 43:1–3

DEAR HEAVENLY FATHER,
your care is all encompassing.
It misses no aspect of my
need. It knows where I am
weak and covers my vulnera-
bility. It shelters me against
the elements of life and brings
me safely home. I am not
afraid because you have saved
me and have adopted me as
your own. Your love is my
salvation. Amen.

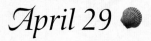

I praise you, for I am fearfully and wonderfully made. Wonderful are your works; that I know very well.

PSALM 139:14

I'M GLAD YOU'VE made me, Lord. Thank you for the qualities I like most about myself, things you've built in that make me feel special. Help me remember these positives during those times when others put me down or when I'm feeling down about myself. Teach me to accept myself, my whole self—weaknesses, warts, and all—remembering that I am a work in progress, created by your hand and being recreated within by your love.

No one can make you feel inferior without your consent.

—ELEANOR ROOSEVELT

April 30

Jesus said, "Those who find their life will lose it, and those who lose their life for my sake will find it."

MATTHEW 10:39

O DIVINE MASTER, grant that I may not so much seek
To be consoled as to console,
To be understood as to understand,
To be loved as to love;
For it is in giving that we receive;
It is in pardoning that we are pardoned;
It is in dying that we are born to eternal life.

—ST. FRANCIS OF ASSISI

Jesus' life reveals this fantastic irony: Only the road of humble service leads us to true greatness.

My prayer life:

_____

_____

_____

_____

_____

_____

_____

_____

_____

_____

_____

_____

_____

May 1

There is no fear in love, but perfect love casts out fear;... We love because he first loved us.

1 JOHN 4:18–19

YOUR LOVE is perfect, God. It surprises me, loving me when I feel unlovable, reaching out to me when I least believe it will. It delights me, showing me secrets and insights, as well as wonders and joys. It challenges me, coaxing me to keep trying and pressing me toward new achievements. It disciplines me, correcting my errors while leading me back toward truth. It keeps me safe when life gets rough and holds me close whenever I long to be comforted. Your love is perfect, and I always want to stay in the middle of it. Keep me there, I pray. Amen.

Do all things without murmuring and arguing, so that you may be blameless and innocent, children of God.

PHILIPPIANS 2:14–15

*F*ATHER, how holy and great is your promise. You've been so good to us, but somehow, Father, we find things about which to complain even though we've been given life eternal. Renew our vision; help us to see heaven. Help us to be busy about the right business—the business of serving you.

—*THE INSPIRATIONAL STUDY BIBLE*

When our focus is on the Lord, our problems cannot impair our vision.

May 3

*The [Samaritan] woman said to [Jesus],
"Sir, ... Are you greater than our ancestor
Jacob, who gave us the well, and with his
sons and his flocks drank from it?"*

JOHN 4:11–12

$\mathcal{G}$OD, sometimes I have doubts and questions about issues of faith. I'm not always sure where to voice these, but I feel the need to find answers, or at least to talk with someone about them. Thank you for being my safe place to talk about them. Lead me to other people of faith who do not feel threatened by my questions and who will be faithful to the truth.

**Never discourage a sincere question—honest
doubt is better than dishonest faith.**

—JANETTE OKE, *THE FATHER OF LOVE*

He was despised and rejected by others; a man of suffering and acquainted with infirmity; and as one from whom others hide their faces he was despised, and we held him of no account.

ISAIAH 53:3

JESUS, You know what rejection feels like, and I do too. When those times come, may I turn to You.... And when I think about rejections in the past, help me to trust in Your steadfast love for me, Your perfect plan for my life, and Your power to redeem the bad in my life.... Help me to forgive where I need to forgive...and, when I am tempted to reject someone, may I instead extend Your love. Amen.

—BOB BARNES, *15 MINUTES ALONE WITH GOD FOR MEN*

When I rejected God, he loved me
in return and received me back.
Now when people reject me, I
pray I can be as forgiving as God.

 *May 5*

We know that all things work together for good for those who love God, who are called according to his purpose.

ROMANS 8:28

*L*ORD, I'm so flawed. I make so many mistakes and so many bad choices. Sometimes I don't understand how anything good can come from my life. But then I remember that your miracle of grace is at work in me, transforming me, changing my foolish and self-centered ways, and turning these messes I often make into a masterpiece of your design. Thank you for accepting me as I am and for loving me enough not to leave me that way.

When you bake a cake, you put in raw flour, baking powder, soda, bitter chocolate, shortening, etc., none of which taste very good in themselves, but which work together to make a delicious cake. And so with our sins and our mistakes—although they are not good in themselves, if we commit them in honest, simple faith to the Lord, He will work them out His own way and in His own time make something of them for our good and His glory.

—BILLY GRAHAM, *UNTO THE HILLS*

Take delight in the Lord, and he will give you the desires of your heart. Commit your way to the Lord; trust in him, and he will act.
PSALM 37:4–5

LORD, may my desires change to your desires. Lord, if a desire is good and profitable, give me grace to fulfill it to your glory. But if it be hurtful and injurious to my soul's health, then remove it from my mind.
—THOMAS Á KEMPIS

Sometimes my mother used to tell me that I didn't know what was good for me: such as when I wanted too much candy, when I didn't want to brush my teeth, when I complained about going to bed early on a school night, and when I wanted to skip the vegetables and get right to the dessert. Now, in retrospect, I see that she was right. Similarly, God's ways are sometimes opposite of what I want to do, but it is always in my best interest–always what's good for me–to obey his parental advice.
—CHRISTINE DALLMAN

May 7

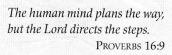

The human mind plans the way,
but the Lord directs the steps.
PROVERBS 16:9

LORD, sometimes I hold on to the controls too tightly. Help me loosen my grip and trust that you will faithfully guide me in the best way. When my desire to make something happen consumes me, and when I try to manipulate people and circumstances to achieve a desired outcome, help me pause, take a deep breath, and ask for your help in breaking this pattern of behavior. I know you are faithful and capable of handling each and every situation; help me rest in that truth. Amen.

Significant living is more about the art of steering, than the tedious task of mastering. You prepare, you plan, you strategize, and then you go out and take it as it comes.
—CHARLIE HEDGES, *GETTING THE RIGHT THINGS RIGHT*

May 8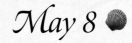

I have given skill to all the skillful, so that they may make all that I have commanded you.

EXODUS 31:6

O THOU WHO ART the all-pervading glory of the world, we bless thee for the power of beauty to gladden our hearts. We praise thee that even the least of us may feel a thrill of thy creative joy when we give form and substance to our thoughts and, beholding our handiwork, find it good and fair.

—WALTER RAUSCHENBUSCH

Our ability to create is evidence that our Creator loves to share with us the pleasures and wonders of his own powers and abilities.

 *May 9*

*Bear one another's burdens, and in this
way you will fulfill the law of Christ.*
GALATIANS 6:2

*G*OD, sometimes it's easier to find fault
with the people around me than it is to
find reasons to praise them. But when I
stop and think of all the ways in which
you encourage me (even during those
times when I'm making mistakes left and
right), I realize how much we all need to
be uplifted and carried along from time to
time. Remind me of the power of a positive word, and grant me the kindness and
sensitivity to give sincere encouragement
whenever and wherever it's needed.

**Let us no more contend, nor blame
Each other, blam'd enough elsewhere, but strive
In offices of love, how we may lighten
Each other's burden, in our share of woe.**

—JOHN MILTON

May 10

*The Lord will keep you from all evil; he
will keep your life. The Lord will keep
your going out and your coming in from
this time on and forevermore.*

PSALM 121:7–8

MAY THE ROAD rise to meet you,
May the wind be always at your back,
May the sun shine warm on your face,
The rain fall softly on your fields;
And until we meet again,
May God hold you in the palm of his hand.

—TRADITIONAL IRISH PRAYER

**Though life is full of danger, of unexpected difficulty, and of
unwelcome turmoil, the one unchanging reality remains in
which we may find all comfort and blessing: God is near.**

May 11

LORD, help me maintain my sense of
humor today, even when things get tense.
There's enough gloom and doom in the
world; I want to introduce some happiness
and a bit of laughter into it all. Please give me
a light heart and an optimistic outlook to set
the tone for those whom I will influence.
Bring your light of joy into my life and let it
shine through what I do and say today.

**Don't get your knickers in a
knot. Nothing is solved and it
just makes you walk funny.**
—KATHRYN CARPENTER

May 12

They refused to obey...they stiffened their necks....But you are a God ready to forgive, gracious and merciful, slow to anger and abounding in steadfast love, and you did not forsake them.

NEHEMIAH 9:17

THE PEOPLE AROUND ME are driving me nuts, God. Traffic was backed up on the tollway, the checkout counters were flooded with carts and strange characters, and the sidewalks were crowded and crunched. My mood overtook my manners today, and I stubbornly refused to say "after you," "excuse me," and "please" until I heard a three-year-old in the parking lot say politely to her mother, "Thank you." With an apology on my lips, help me climb out of this rut of irritation and shame and make amends. Help me learn from my mistakes and do better for the rest of this day.

May 13

Though the fig tree does not blossom, and no fruit is on the vines; though the produce of the olive fails and the fields yield no food; though the flock is cut off from the fold and there is no herd in the stalls, yet I will rejoice in the Lord; I will exult in the God of my salvation.

HABAKKUK 3:17–18

Murphy's law sometimes seems to characterize my life, God, but I don't want to have a defeatist attitude. You allow difficulties to come my way to refine my character. Help me see setbacks as challenges and not as curses. Help me approach problems as opportunities to learn and grow and not as insurmountable walls. Teach me to have a tenacity of faith that can find a reason to be happy, even in adversity. Amen.

'Tis easy enough to be pleasant,
When life flows along like a song;
But the man worth while is the one who will smile
When everything goes dead wrong.

—ELLA WHEELER COX, "WORTH WHILE"

Beloved, we are God's children now; what we will be has not yet been revealed. What we do know is this: when he is revealed, we will be like him, for we will see him as he is. And all who have this hope in him purify themselves, just as he is pure.

1 JOHN 3:2–3

LORD, GRANT US eyes to see
Within the seed a tree,
Within the glowing egg a bird,
Within the shroud a butterfly:
Till taught by such, we see
Beyond all creatures thee,
And hearken for thy tender word
And hear it, "Fear not; it is I."

—CHRISTINA ROSSETTI

God's tender transformation of our fearful hearts into faith-filled ones is a miracle no less significant than any other.

May 15

*You desire truth in the inward being;
therefore teach me wisdom in my
secret heart.*

PSALM 51:6

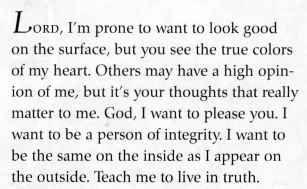

*L*ORD, I'm prone to want to look good
on the surface, but you see the true colors
of my heart. Others may have a high opinion of me, but it's your thoughts that really
matter to me. God, I want to please you. I
want to be a person of integrity. I want to
be the same on the inside as I appear on
the outside. Teach me to live in truth.

The temptation of the age is to look good without being good.
—BRENNAN MANNING, *THE RAGAMUFFIN GOSPEL*

Submit yourselves therefore to God. Resist the devil, and he will flee from you. Draw near to God, and he will draw near to you.

JAMES 4:7–8

𝐹ATHER GOD, You know I feel distant from You, but I know that I'm the one who moved. I've been trying to be the captain of my ship, but it's not working. I want to get back with Your program. I want You to shape me into the person You have designed me to be, and I want to work with You. I want to be malleable in Your hands. Amen.

—BOB BARNES, *15 MINUTES ALONE WITH GOD FOR MEN*

On your journey through life, if you stick close to God, you can't go wrong. As an expert conductor, his train is always on the right track; as an expert pilot, his flight is always on time; and as an expert captain, his ship always finds safe harbor.

May 17

I have been young, and now am old, yet I have not seen the righteous forsaken or their children begging bread.

PSALM 37:25

𝒢OD OF MY LIFE, how often I have turned to you through the years. How faithful a friend you have proven to be. I could never hope to find a more kind and true companion. I see now that life passes quickly and that the old age I never imagined would come to me is coming. But it does not frighten me, Lord, because you are here. I look forward to the coming years. I look forward to growing older and wiser still. For the wiser I become, the more I understand your ways and the more I grow to love you. Remain with me always, dear God, and I will delight in each day you give me. Amen.

Grow old along with me!
The best is yet to be,
The last of life for which the first was made.

—ROBERT BROWNING

May 18

Purge me with hyssop, and I shall be clean; wash me, and I shall be whiter than snow.... Create in me a clean heart, O God, and put a new and right spirit within me.

PSALM 51:7, 10

LORD, YOU CAN DO everything. We beg you to take pity on us, making us not merely listen to what you say, but put it into practice also. Send the flood of your waters over our souls, destroying within us what should be destroyed, and giving life to that which should live.

—ORIGEN

Good news for imperfect people: God is very much in the business of clean slates, fresh starts, and happy endings.

May 19

Whatever your hand finds to do, do with your might.... Follow the inclination of your heart and the desire of your eyes, but know that for all these things God will bring you into judgment.

ECCLESIASTES 9:10; 11:9

HEAVENLY FATHER, thank you for the freedom to pursue my dreams and goals. As I continuously embark on the many and varied adventures of this life, keep my heart tuned into your ways so that whatever I do and wherever I go, I'll honor you. For, Lord, I want to live in such a way that when my days on earth draw near an end, not only will I have lived fully, but also I will have conducted myself in a way that has pleased you.

Adventure is worthwhile in itself.
—AMELIA EARHART

Then I heard the voice of the Lord saying, "Whom shall I send, and who will go for us?" And I said, "Here am I; send me!"

ISAIAH 6:8

*D*EAR LORD, you have spoken to me, and I have heard your call. Now I need your strength to be obedient to your will. Fill me with your Spirit so that I might please and glorify you in all that I do. Amen.

A small rudder can turn a great ship. A tiny spark can set a forest aflame. May God grant me the grace, as I walk with him, to make a positive difference in my world.

May 21

A good name is to be chosen rather than great riches, and favor is better than silver or gold.

PROVERBS 22:1

How WILL MY FAMILY remember me many years from now, dear Lord? What kind of a person will they say I was? How will they describe my relationships? What will they say about my character? O God, I want to leave a legacy of goodness. I want to leave a path that my children and grandchildren can follow. Help me today to blaze that trail, to make it clear and wide, and to mark it well.

The erection of a monument is superfluous; our memory will endure if our lives have deserved it.

—PLINY THE YOUNGER

May 22

Now the Lord is the Spirit, and where the
Spirit of the Lord is, there is freedom.

2 CORINTHIANS 3:17

O MAKER MY MAKER! my hope is in thee.
My Jesus, dear Savior! now set my soul free.
From this my hard prison, my spirit uprisen,
Soars upward to thee.
Thus moaning and groaning, and bending the knee,
I adore, and implore that thou liberate me.

—MARY, QUEEN OF SCOTS

Though my body be locked up in the darkest
dungeon, my spirit soars where it will, and
none can keep it from communing with its
Maker—from whom it came, to whom it lives,
and in whom it exists forever.

May 23

*See what love the Father has given
us, that we should be called children
of God; and that is what we are.*

1 JOHN 3:1

TIME AND TIME AGAIN, heavenly Father,
I'm amazed at the depth of your love for
me. I don't think I will ever entirely understand or comprehend it, but I am so
pleased to be so loved. It seems that your
love for me just keeps getting stronger.
When I think I must have exhausted your
love, it reaches out again and gives itself to
me. When I think I must have come to the
end of your love, it encompasses me and
I am swallowed up by it. I'm lost in
it…found in it. Your love is where I will
always belong. It's my safe place, my home.

For God so loved the world that he gave his only Son, so that everyone who believes in him may not perish but may have eternal life.

JOHN 3:16

*D*EAR LORD, it seems that you are so madly in love with your creatures that you could not live without us. So you created us; and then, when we turned away from you, you redeemed us. Yet you are God, and so have no need of us. Your greatness is made no greater by our creation; your power is made no stronger by our redemption. You have no duty to care for us, no debt to re-pay us. It is love, and love alone, which moves you.

—CATHERINE OF SIENA

I've never been so loved by man, woman, or child as by God. Indeed, he gave the very best— his Son—so I could become one of his children.

May 25

For in Christ Jesus you are all children of God through faith. As many of you as were baptized into Christ have clothed yourselves with Christ. There is no longer Jew or Greek, there is no longer slave or free, there is no longer male and female; for all of you are one in Christ Jesus.

GALATIANS 3:26–28

CREATOR OF ALL PEOPLE, sometimes I become so focused on the differences that exist between me and those around me that I forget how very much we have in common. Of course, we all need food, water, and shelter, but we also long for kindness, love, and attention. Each of us wants to be acknowledged and valued for who we are. Help me, Lord, to treat all people with the respect they deserve as your priceless creations. Remind me that you gave your life for each one and that to each one, you unfailingly extend your love. Teach me to emulate your goodness.

May 26

For I am convinced that neither death, nor life, nor angels, nor rulers, nor things present, nor things to come, nor powers, nor height, nor depth, nor anything else in all creation, will be able to separate us from the love of God in Christ Jesus our Lord.

ROMANS 8:38–39

EVERYTHING AROUND ME keeps changing, Lord. Nothing lasts. My moods shift; the seasons of life come and go; and friends become different. While I age physically, my face is different than it was ten years ago. But when I start to feel as if there is nothing sure and steady on which I can depend, I realize that even as I contemplate these things, your love—your ever-present, unchanging love—is holding me close to your heart. Through the transitions of life, your love keeps me sane and gives me courage and hope for the future. Your love is my rock, my anchor, and my foundation.

So the love of the God who is spirit is no fitful, fluctuating thing, as human love is, nor is it a mere impotent longing for things that may never be; it is, rather, a spontaneous determination of God's whole being in an attitude of benevolence and benefaction, an attitude freely chosen and firmly fixed.

—J. I. PACKER, *KNOWING GOD*

May 27

*Examine yourselves to see whether you
are living in the faith. Test yourselves.*
2 CORINTHIANS 13:5

LORD, I must admit that I'm quick to assume that a
mistake or a problem is someone else's fault. I don't like
to admit it when I'm wrong. I am slow to think that I
could be responsible for something that has gone wrong.
God, forgive me for being afraid of losing face. Please
help me learn how to admit my shortcomings without
feeling that all is lost when I do. Amen.

**Alarms serve a purpose. They signal a problem.
Sometimes the problem is out there. More
often it's in here. So before you peek outside,
take a good look inside.**

—MAX LUCADO, *WHEN GOD WHISPERS YOUR NAME*

Do not neglect to show hospitality to strangers, for by doing that some have entertained angels without knowing it.

HEBREWS 13:2

*P*EACE BE to this house
And to all who dwell in it.
Peace be to them that enter
And to them that depart. Amen.

—*A CHILD'S BOOK OF PRAYERS*

The best hospitality is found with those who offer the blessing of welcome as you enter, the blessing of peace while you're there, and the blessing of farewell as you leave.

By faith Abraham obeyed when he was called to set out for a place that he was to receive as an inheritance; and he set out, not knowing where he was going. By faith he stayed for a time in the land he had been promised.

HEBREWS 11:8–9

LORD, if Abraham could follow you through a major change in his life, so can I. Grant me, Lord, the courage and vision of Abraham. Build my faith through this experience of stepping out without having all the details nailed down. I want to do the right thing, but I need clarification from you as to what that might be. Please show me the difference between a foolish decision and a faithful decision, and help me act on the faith you've given me.

Setting down roots in a new place can seem to threaten our survival. But given enough time, it usually allows us more room to expand.
—VIVIAN ELISABETH GLYCK, *LIFE I LEARNED FROM MY GARDEN*

Render service with enthusiasm, as to the Lord and not to men and women, knowing that whatever good we do, we will receive the same again from the Lord.

EPHESIANS 6:7–8

FATHER GOD, SEARCH ME and show me my motivation for what I do. Forgive my selfishness. Give me a pure heart that joyfully and energetically serves You, the Author and Giver of life. Help me serve with my eyes on You and not on other people, hoping they'll notice what I do. And thank You for the gracious and generous rewards You promise even when our motives aren't pure and our service is imperfect. Amen.

—BOB BARNES, *15 MINUTES ALONE WITH GOD FOR MEN*

The depth of our love and gratitude to God is revealed in the fervency and attentiveness with which we serve others.

May 31

Happy are those whose strength is in you, in whose heart are the highways to Zion. As they go through the valley of Baca they make it a place of springs;... They go from strength to strength.

PSALM 84:5–7

I DO NOT UNDERSTAND why some people must suffer so much pain in this life, heavenly Father. It seems as if there are those who get more than their fair share of hardship. What does it mean? I know it's not a case of your forgetting us, but that's what it feels like. Help me see that where there is suffering, there you are, for you have experienced ultimate suffering, and you suffer with us. Yet, you overcame pain and death, and in your strength I, too, can triumph. Cause me to grow in inner beauty and to learn and become wiser through my struggles. For then, with authenticity and gentleness, I can lead others who are hurting toward your strength and your compassion.

> **O fear not in a world like this,**
> **And thou shalt know ere long,**
> **Know how sublime a thing it is**
> **To suffer and be strong.**
>
> —HENRY WADSWORTH LONGFELLOW,
> "THE LIGHT OF STARS"

My prayer life:

June 1

These are the things that you shall do: Speak the truth to one another, render in your gates judgments that are true and make for peace, do not devise evil in your hearts against one another.

ZECHARAIAH 8:16–17

WHEN I AM TEMPTED to strike out in frustration, anger, or revenge at those around me, Lord, remind me that doing so will only perpetuate the very attitudes and actions I try hard to discourage in those who look to me for guidance. In those emotion-filled moments, I need your strength to back away from the fight. I need your wisdom to keep my mouth from speaking words I will later regret. I need your perspective to see others as people who, like me, need mercy. Bring your peace into my encounters with others. Show me how to maintain that peace no matter how another person may choose to behave toward me. Amen.

*With my whole heart I seek you; do not let me stray from your command-
ments....My soul is consumed with longing for your ordinances at all times.*

PSALM 119:10, 20

ALMIGHTY God
I want to come closer to you,
I want to love you more dearly,
Hear you more clearly
And follow you more nearly.

—WILLIAM H. SHANNON, *SILENCE ON FIRE*

**Whenever we seek to get close to God, our move-
ment toward him is, indeed, a homeward journey.**

June 3

*Better is a handful with quiet than two
handfuls with toil, and a chasing after wind.*
ECCLESIASTES 4:6

 ℋEAVENLY FATHER, as I look at how I spend my time,
I see where my priorities lie. In my heart and in my
intentions, I have one set of priorities. In my actual living,
though, another set of priorities is revealed. You know
that sometimes I say yes to commitments and obligations
that steal my time from things I value most. Help me not
play the part of a victim when it comes to my schedule.
Show me how to take responsibility for the life you've
given me by exercising the power of choice. Help me
wield the words *yes* and *no* wisely and judiciously so that
I won't look back and experience the regret of squander-
ing precious, irretrievable opportunities to do the things
in life that are truly important.

**We've been taught to accelerate in order to
accomplish more. Maybe it's time to realize
that pushing harder and faster wears out our
bodies. Deceleration will help us handle our
time in a better way.**

—H. NORMAN WRIGHT, *SIMPLIFY YOUR LIFE*

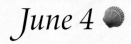

June 4

You are the light of the world.... No one after lighting a lamp puts it under the bushel basket, but on the lampstand, and it gives light to all in the house. In the same way, let your light shine before others.

MATTHEW 5:14–16

J ESUS,... Help me to realize in the course of this day and tomorrow who I am and who You are, what I represent and what my witness is about. And take care of me. I love You.

—ANDREW M. GREELEY, *LOVE AFFAIR*

When I aspire to become a person whom others can emulate–in word, action, and attitude–my experience is enriched, not only by the benefits I reap from a wholesome lifestyle but also by the people who move closer to wholeness because they have been encouraged and inspired by my example.

June 5

We are ambassadors for Christ, since God is making his appeal through us; we entreat you on behalf of Christ, be reconciled to God.

2 CORINTHIANS 5:20

LORD, sometimes I feel as if my larger purpose gets lost in the shuffle of life. I start to look at my daily accomplishments and wonder how valuable they are. When I don't feel a clear purpose or direction in my relationships, tasks, and activities, I need you to remind me that one of the most meaningful things I can do in this life is to point others toward you and your love.

June 6

*Do you not know that you are God's temple
and that God's Spirit dwells in you?*

1 CORINTHIANS 3:16

DEAR LORD, we are your temple made
by your hands. Help us to honor you and
give you the glory by letting your Spirit
live in us and continue to transform us into
the people you want us to be. Thank you
for blessing us with the lives you have
given us. These things, we pray. Amen.

**What an honor that the God of the universe
prefers to dwell not in beautiful synagogues,
exquisite cathedrals, or fancy church buildings
but rather within our very selves!**

June 7

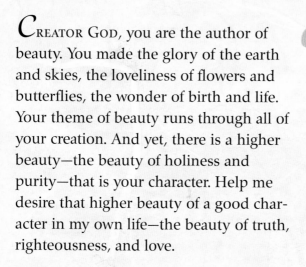

*Charm is deceitful, and beauty is vain, but a
woman who fears the Lord is to be praised.*
PROVERBS 31:30

CREATOR GOD, you are the author of
beauty. You made the glory of the earth
and skies, the loveliness of flowers and
butterflies, the wonder of birth and life.
Your theme of beauty runs through all of
your creation. And yet, there is a higher
beauty—the beauty of holiness and
purity—that is your character. Help me
desire that higher beauty of a good character in my own life—the beauty of truth,
righteousness, and love.

**The pursuit of beauty is much more dangerous nonsense than
the pursuit of truth or goodness, because it affords a stronger
temptation to the ego.**

—NORTHROP FRYE, *ANATOMY OF CRITICISM*

For you did not receive a spirit of slavery to fall back into fear, but you have received a spirit of adoption. When we cry, "Abba! Father!" it is that very Spirit bearing witness with our spirit that we are children of God.

ROMANS 8:15–16

OH GOD, you conceived us.
We are your children….
Lead us out of the void, out of destructiveness, out of the swirling storm. If we stumble, pick us up. Carry us when we can't walk, and teach us your ways. Let us be born as you intended. For all goodness is yours, and your love endures forever.
Amen.

—BILL WILLIAMS, *NAKED BEFORE GOD*

Just as children seek to imitate their parents, God's children try to imitate the goodness and righteousness of their heavenly Father.

June 9

Do not judge, so that you may not be judged....how can you say to your neighbor, "Let me take the speck out of your eye," while the log is in your own eye?

MATTHEW 7:1, 4

Too much criticism, Lord, will poison the relationships I enjoy. Help me not nag or put people down when they make mistakes. Instead, let me remember my own fallibility as I encounter flaws in others. Help me remember that we are all works in progress, people whom you are patiently correcting and nurturing toward spiritual maturity. Grant me an ample measure of your mercy, grace, patience, encouragement, and love when I'm with my family, friends, neighbors, and coworkers.

Be not angry that you cannot make others as you wish them to be, since you cannot make yourself as you wish to be.

—THOMAS Á KEMPIS

June 10

God has not left himself without a witness in doing
good—giving you rains from heaven and fruitful seasons,
and filling you with food and your hearts with joy.

ACTS 14:17

*A*LMIGHTY GOD, we thank you for making the earth fruitful, so that it might
produce what is needed for life: Bless
those who work in the fields; give us
seasonable weather; and grant that we
may all share the fruits of the earth,
rejoicing in your goodness.

—*THE BOOK OF COMMON PRAYER*

**This summer, recognize that
the growing season is a miracle of God's power and a
demonstration of his kindness. Marvel at heightening
stalks in a corn field, an
orchard of ripening fruit, and
a sea of wheat that stretches
over the landscape. Give
praise and thanks to God for
the meals you enjoy today.**

June 11

*Every generous act of giving, with every perfect gift, is
from above, coming down from the Father of lights, with
whom there is no variation or shadow due to change.*

JAMES 1:17

GRACIOUS FATHER, the gifts that flow from your good
heart into my life capture my attention and fill me with
joy. But I wonder how often I turn my blessing-enamored
gaze toward you? Not often enough, Lord. Not as often as
I wish I did. But today I will focus on you, listen to you,
and enjoy your nearness. Today, I will remember that
you are my ultimate blessing. Amen.

**While you look at what is
given, look also at the giver.**

—SENECA

It was fitting that God, for whom and through whom all things exist, in bringing many children to glory, should make the pioneer of their salvation perfect through sufferings.... Because he himself was tested by what he suffered, he is able to help those who are being tested.

HEBREWS 2:10, 18

*H*EAVENLY FATHER, I recall how your Son had to suffer in order to set me free from sin and death. I pray that what I now suffer will increase my faith and help me to be more compassionate. Strengthen me and empower me with the Holy Spirit so I can be a beacon of love to others despite the tests I now face.

The presence of our compassionate God is made more meaningful when we realize that he, too, has suffered and now walks with us through our own sufferings, leading us toward eternal joy.

June 13

Whoever loves pleasure will suffer want;... Whoever pursues righteousness and kindness will find life and honor.

PROVERBS 21:17, 21

LORD JESUS, your goal for me is not mere personal happiness but holiness. You want to show me the way to true, inner satisfaction, which does not come through temporal pleasures and a carefree existence. In fact, the opposite is often true: Some of the happiest people have endured difficulty, pain, and hardship along their way. I know with you by my side, I'll find peace and true happiness through the good and the bad.

June 14

So let us not grow weary in doing what is right, for we will reap at harvest time, if we do not give up. So then, whenever we have an opportunity, let us work for the good of all.
GALATIANS 6:9–10

$\mathcal{P}$USHING ON PAST the fear and struggle, Lord, I find a second wind of faith while you cheer me on. What would I do without your encouragement and without your tender mercies that lift me up when I get too tired and the load I bear seems too heavy for me? You always lighten my load and carry my burden when I call on you. Thanks for giving me an extra measure of grace for this day. You're my dearest friend and companion. I love you.

Sometimes it feels like I can't catch my breath between life's lessons, running and straining to keep up. But if I hold tight, buoyed by God's strength, I can fly.

—HEIDI WALDROP BAY, *WOMANSPIRIT*

June 15

You who live in the shelter of the Most High,
who abide in the shadow of the Almighty, will
say to the Lord, "My refuge and my fortress; my
God, in whom I trust."

PSALM 91:1–2

*T*HROUGH ALL my Life thy Favor is
So frankly shew'd to me
That in thy House for evermore
My dwelling-place shall be.

—JOHN BUNYAN, *THE PILGRIM'S PROGRESS*

To live a life of faith is to live
always in God's presence, at
peace in the home of his love.

June 16

God is love, and those who abide in love abide in God, and God abides in them.... those who love God must love their brothers and sisters also.
1 JOHN 4:16, 21

WHEN I THINK ABOUT your example of love, dear God, I realize that love is far more than a warm emotion. It is a deep commitment to look out for another's best interest, even at my own expense. That kind of commitment scares me, though, Lord. What if someone takes advantage of my love? What if I get hurt? But that's the risk of love, isn't it? To experience true love in a relationship, I must be willing to put my pride and my heart on the line. Protect me, Lord, as I venture out today with love as my goal.

June 17

Let the favor of the Lord our God be upon us, and prosper for us the work of our hands—O prosper the work of our hands.

PSALM 90:17

MY GOD, since You are with me, and since it is Your will that I should apply my mind to these outward things, I pray that You will give me the grace to remain with You and keep company with You. But so that my work may be better, Lord, work with me; receive my work and possess all my affections. Amen.

—BROTHER LAWRENCE, *THE PRACTICE OF THE PRESENCE OF GOD*

It is those times when no one else is watching us that our work reflects the true quality of our character.

June 18

We who are strong ought to put up with the failings of the weak, and not to please ourselves. Each of us must please our neighbor for the good purpose of building up the neighbor.

ROMANS 15:1–2

LORD JESUS, when the man came to you asking you to define "neighbor" for him, you told the story of the good Samaritan. By that parable, you've made it clear that our neighbor is anyone who is in need, anyone we happen to meet who requires our help. Open my eyes to the neighbors around me today, Lord, and show me how you would have me reach out in love to encourage them.

I hope that you'll remember, even when you're feeling blue, that it's you I like, it's you yourself, it's you.

—FRED ROGERS (MISTER ROGERS)

June 19

For it was you who formed my inward parts; you knit me together in my mother's womb.... My frame was not hidden from you, when I was being made in secret, intricately woven in the depths of the earth. Your eyes beheld my unformed substance. In your book were written all the days that were formed for me, when none of them as yet existed. How weighty to me are your thoughts, O God! How vast is the sum of them!

PSALM 139:13, 15–17

O GOD, who made me absolutely unique, help me to value more the person You made me to be. Protect me from comparisons and envy and discouragement over what I am not. Inspire me to become more the person that I am and that I should be. Grant that I may understand that You love me, faults and all, and that I may accept myself even as you accept me. I ask this in the name of Jesus the Lord. Amen.

—ANDREW M. GREELEY, *LOVE AFFAIR*

To be alive, to be the only one who ever was or will be just like me, is an amazing opportunity, filled with limitless possibilities. Let me learn more and more to enjoy just being me!

June 20

Be strong and courageous; do not be frightened or dismayed, for the Lord your God is with you wherever you go.
JOSHUA 1:9

I NEVER KNOW, God, when I might be called upon to act bravely, to step up and seize a moment that passes before me at a critical juncture in life. Help me stay near you, heavenly Father, so that during times when my knees would normally go weak, my heart would race out of control, and my mind would go blank, I can turn to you in faith and be made courageous by your strong intervention.

June 21

May the Lord, maker of heaven and earth, bless you from Zion.

PSALM 134:3

GOD, THANK YOU for blessing me with your joy. My life is so full of your goodness that I want to share this happiness I feel with everyone I meet today. Please bless these people with your joy. This I pray. Amen.

Joy is contagious. When we are joyful people, we bless all who meet us, know us, and love us.

He will speak to this people, to
whom he has said, "This is rest; give
rest to the weary; and this is repose."
ISAIAH 28:11–12

SLOW ME DOWN TODAY, Lord! Help me
remember to visit the break room, to step
away from the frenzy of the demands of the
day, to talk with you, and to close my eyes
and breathe deeply long enough to calm my
frayed nerves. You are the inventor of rest,
and you prescribe it for all who live on earth.
I need that daily dose of reprieve. Help me
take it and be blessed by it.

We go through life like a video player on fast-forward.
What about the other buttons: play and pause?
—H. NORMAN WRIGHT, *SIMPLIFY YOUR LIFE*

June 23

*Jesus Christ is the same yesterday
and today and forever.*

HEBREWS 13:8

GREAT IS THY faithfulness, O God my Father,
There is no shadow of turning with Thee;
Thou changest not, Thy compassions they fail not;
As Thou hast been, Thou forever wilt be.
Great is Thy faithfulness! Great is Thy faithfulness!
Morning by morning new mercies I see;
All I have needed Thy hand hath provided—
Great is Thy faithfulness, Lord, unto me!

—THOMAS O. CHISHOLM, "GREAT IS THY FAITHFULNESS"

**In a world of continual and relentless change—some
good and some bad—we can take comfort in knowing
that God does not change, and he is always good.**

You must understand this, my beloved: let everyone be quick to listen, slow to speak, slow to anger;…

JAMES 1:19

*T*ODAY, HEAVENLY FATHER, you may call upon me to listen to someone and hear that person's heart. It may be someone who needs to feel significant enough to be heard, or perhaps someone who is lonely and longs to be connected to another person, or maybe someone who is hurting and needs a sympathetic ear. Whatever the case, Lord, please open my ears so I may listen to someone today. Amen.

It is God's love for us that He not only gives us His Word but also lends us His ear. So it is His work that we do for our brother when we learn to listen to him.

—DIETRICH BONHOEFFER, *LIFE TOGETHER*

June 25

Come to me, all you that are weary and
are carrying heavy burdens, and I will
give you rest.... learn from me; for I am
gentle and humble in heart, and you will
find rest for your souls.

MATTHEW 11:28–29

I FIND MY LIFE so busy, Lord,
That's why I find it so hard
to take out time just for You.
You know all the excuses I have:
Responsibilities to my family,
My work, my health, my need to relax.
There are so many things I have to do
That I am hesitant to add one more thing.

—WILLIAM H. SHANNON, *SILENCE ON FIRE*

Remind me again, Lord, that rest and relaxation
are a cure for many of the maladies that diminish
my effectiveness. Frustration, anger, weariness,
anxiety, susceptibility to illness, lack of focus, and
forgetfulness are all symptoms of my not getting
the rest I need. Please make a way for me to get
adequate sleep and the breaks I need to rejuvenate
and return to my work refreshed.

June 26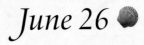

*So teach us to count our days that we
may gain a wise heart.*

PSALM 90:12

*H*EAVENLY FATHER, sometimes I am so
busy looking ahead and anticipating the
future or looking behind and recalling the
past that I miss today's opportunities. Help
me remember that today is the future I've
waited for and the past I will look back
on; you have brought it to me right now
as a moment for living. Therefore, as I
make my decisions as to how to spend
this day, let me feel the power and significance of this here-and-now gift of life.

June 27

You have heard that it was said, "You shall love your neighbor and hate your enemy." But I say to you, Love your enemies and pray for those who persecute you, so that you may be children of your Father in heaven; for he makes his sun rise on the evil and on the good, and sends rain on the righteous and on the unrighteous.

MATTHEW 5:43–45

O GOD, the Father of all, whose Son commanded us to love our enemies: Lead them and us from prejudice to truth; deliver them and us from hatred, cruelty, and revenge; and in your good time enable us all to stand reconciled before you; through Jesus Christ our Lord. Amen.

—THE BOOK OF COMMON PRAYER

The biggest challenge we will face with our enemies is not in making them see things our way but in seeing our way to truly love them.

Brothers and sisters, join in imitating me, and observe those who live according to the example you have in us.

PHILIPPIANS 3:17

God, THANK YOU for the people, past and present, who inspire me to reach out for what is right and good...and even great! Help me to not lose heart when I stumble. Remind me that even my heroes have failed at times. But, Lord, I know that when I am willing to try again, you will lift me up and get me back on track. Help me keep moving forward and reaching out for worthy goals. And grant me the kind of success that makes a mark—an example others can safely and honorably follow.

 *June 29*

In the heavens he has set a tent for the sun, which comes out like a bridegroom from his wedding canopy, and like a strong man runs its course with joy.

PSALM 19:4–5

SUMMER VISITS US AGAIN, Lord, and I am ready for the long, warm days that tempt the children to run through lawn sprinklers and signal the return of the ice-cream truck driver to his customary route through our neighborhood. The trees are garbed again in the classic fashion, and every morning now, I hear the birds conversing outside, before my clock's alarm even goes off. Summer seems to personify joy, heavenly Father, and you must know how much we need to be lifted up in our spirits, for each year you've devoted an entire season to encouraging us. Thank you for this time of joy.

What is so rare as a day in June?
    Then, if ever, come perfect days;
Then Heaven tries the earth if it be in tune,
    And over it softly her warm ear lays.
—JAMES RUSSELL LOWELL, "THE VISION OF SIR LAUNFAL"

At midnight I rise to praise you [Lord], because of your righteous ordinances.
I am a companion of all who fear you, of those who keep your precepts.

PSALM 119:62–63

*T*HERE ARE TIMES, Lord, when it is good for me to be alone with you, to contemplate my life, to reaffirm my need for you and your care for me, and to listen to your heartbeat. I need to be quiet, for in quietness I find you. But there are also times when I need to be immersed in community, to have vital connections with those around me, to feel their needs, and to share my own needs with them. I need to be in fellowship, for in community I also find you.

Let him who is not in community
beware of being alone.
—DIETRICH BONHOEFFER, *LIFE TOGETHER*

My prayer life:

_____

_____

_____

_____

_____

_____

_____

_____

_____

_____

_____

_____

_____

July 1

You do not even know what tomorrow will bring.
JAMES 4:14

LORD, I spend too much time thinking about the next day, the next week, the next year. Stop me, please, and fix my attention on today, *this* day. What are my attitudes like today? Are my words lifting others up or beating them down? Have I taken the opportunity to help someone? Have I become a little more like you today? I don't want to put myself on a guilt trip, Lord; I just want to be reminded that today is where life is happening. Help me be ready for the opportunities to love.

Our problem is not needing to know the truth about tomorrow; it's needing to live the truth we know today.
—CHARLES R. SWINDOLL, *THE FINISHING TOUCH*

July 2

The Lord is the stronghold of my life; of whom shall I be afraid?…Though an army encamp against me, my heart shall not fear; though war rise up against me, yet I will be confident.
PSALM 27:1, 3

GOD, I understand why you are calling me, but I don't like conflict. Why doesn't someone else speak up, because I don't know what to say. Conflict makes my stomach sick. I feel defensive and defeated at the same time. I don't want to do battle; I just want to express another point of view. Give me confidence and strength to disagree, Lord. Stand with me so I can stand steadfastly.

The presence of the Lord will empower us to be honest and compassionate so we can be a light to the world and not defeated captives to fear and doubt.

July 3

Where the Spirit of the Lord is, there is freedom.

2 CORINTHIANS 3:17

OUR FATHERS' GOD, to Thee,
Author of liberty,
To Thee we sing;
Long may our land be bright
With freedom's holy light;
Protect us by Thy might,
Great God, our king.

—SAMUEL F. SMITH, "AMERICA"

Freedom is God's idea. It was his idea from the beginning. It's only when we mistrust his intentions and abandon his loving guidance that we find ourselves becoming less free and more enslaved to the tyranny of our own unwise choices.

July 4

As servants of God, live as free people, yet do not use your freedom as a pretext for evil. Honor everyone. Love the family of believers. Fear God.

1 PETER 2:16–17

HEAVENLY FATHER, thank you for the freedoms I enjoy. I cherish these privileges and take seriously my responsibility to preserve them. Help me to live as an example to the people around me as one who loves and protects liberty by treating laws, leaders, and fellow citizens with the love and respect they deserve. And as I do, may I keep the path clear for my children and grandchildren to walk in this same freedom.

July 5

Male and female he created them.
GENESIS 1:27

GOD, you are the one who invented gender. Your intention, I'm sure, was for us to be a team—men and women working together, bringing their unique abilities and strengths to community, helping and encouraging each other. But God, so often we find ourselves at odds, picking apart weaknesses and flaws in the other instead of offering support and friendship. Forgive our selfishness in this. Please help us today to see the opposite sex from your perspective and to act toward them with your love. Amen.

July 6

O give thanks to the Lord, call on his name, make known his deeds among the peoples. Sing to him, sing praises to him; tell of all his wonderful works.

PSALM 105:1–2

*D*EAR LORD, you have filled my heart with so much of your love that I want to sing praises to you and let the world know that you are a great and wonderful God, who has blessed my soul with your supreme joy. Thank you for all that you have done for me. I exalt your name above all names in heaven and on earth. Amen.

My soul can see more clearly than my eyes can, if only I'll let it.

July 7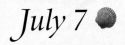

O Lord, who may abide in your tent?
Who may dwell on your holy hill?
Those who walk blamelessly, and do
what is right, and speak the truth
from their heart.

PSALM 15:1–2

TEACH me to walk in honesty, Lord, even when I'm afraid of the truth. I want to be known as someone who can be trusted. But I don't want just a good reputation based on false perceptions; I really want to be what I seem to be. Don't let me get away even with white lies today, heavenly Father. Stop me before I speak and help me choose my words carefully while I boldly, yet lovingly, say it like it is.

An honest man's the noblest work of God.
—ALEXANDER POPE, "ESSAY ON MAN"

 *July 8*

Let me hear what God the Lord will speak, for he will speak peace to his people, to his faithful, to those who turn to him in their hearts.

PSALM 85:8

*F*ATHER. Let me hear You speak. Teach me to recognize Your voice. Create spiritual hunger in me. Cause me to crave Your presence. I open myself to you. Do your work. In Jesus' name.

—JENNIFER KENNEDY DEAN, *POWER PRAYING*

God will always knock before entering. If your heart is open to him today, let him know that. Say it aloud. Ask him to be present with you and to show you what he has in mind for you today. Every day can be an adventure when God leads the way.

Am I now seeking human approval, or God's approval? Or am I trying to please people? If I were still pleasing people, I would not be a servant of Christ.

GALATIANS 1:10

I GET ALL TANGLED UP in this mess of trying to make other people like me, God. In my efforts to get people's approval, I often compromise what I know you would want for me. I realize that this is no way to live, but it's a long-time pattern for me. Show me the way to more healthy relating. Teach me how to focus on pleasing you so I can be free from the tyranny of other people's opinions of me.

Freedom in Christ produces a healthy independence from peer pressure, people-pleasing, and the bondage of human respect.

—BRENNAN MANNING, *THE RAGAMUFFIN GOSPEL*

If we live by the Spirit, let us also be guided by the Spirit.

GALATIANS 5:25

HOLY SPIRIT, the life that gives life.
You are the cause of all movement;
You are the breath of all creatures;
You are the salve that purifies our souls;
You are the ointment that heals our wounds;
You are the fire that warms our hearts;
You are the light that guides our feet.
Let all the world praise you.

—HILDEGARD OF BINGEN

A spiritual journey is best undertaken with the Spirit of God as our guide; for God, who made our spirits, knows the way to finding spiritual wholeness.

July 11

Conduct yourselves honorably . . . so that . . . they may see your honorable deeds and glorify God.

1 PETER 2:12

LORD, I mistakenly think that my day-to-day actions—good or bad—are not significant, but they are. I know that the cumulative effect of my small deeds over a lifetime will certainly influence the people I'm closest to, as well as those with whom I work. I also know that a not-exactly-ethical choice makes a lasting impression on spouses, children, and coworkers. Yet, a wise choice can set someone else on the path of good decision making. One can never know who is watching. Therefore, help me do what's right, Lord. Amen.

Every hair makes its shadow on the ground.

—SPANISH PROVERB

July 12

*The reward for humility and fear of
the Lord is riches and honor and life.*
PROVERBS 22:4

O LORD! Forgive my foolish pride that
seeks to enhance my image. I posture and
pretend in order to impress people I fear
will reject me. Really, God, these efforts
are just lies—exaggerations and illusions I
foolishly make and then desperately try
to maintain. I'm tired of acting this way,
Lord. I'm tired of being afraid of being
found out. Set me free to be who I truly
am. I'm willing to accept whatever losses I
may incur as I seek to gain the peace of
mind that the truth will bring.

July 13

But those who are noble plan noble things, and by noble things they stand.

ISAIAH 32:8

*W*HEN MY GOALS SEEM too small, Lord, when they get swallowed up in feelings of futility, help me seek my larger purpose in life. Help me ask what you have in mind for me while I am here. Show me how to have big goals—goals toward which my day-to-day duties are moving me. And finally, help me to praise you for creating me with a unique purpose and for granting me a meaningful life.

July 14

Precious in the sight of the Lord is the death of his faithful ones.

PSALM 116:15

GRANT, O LORD, to all who are bereaved the spirit of faith and courage, that they may have strength to meet the days to come with steadfastness and patience; not sorrowing as those without hope, but in thankful remembrance of your great goodness, and in the joyful expectation of eternal life with those they love. And this we ask in the name of Jesus Christ our Savior. Amen.

—*THE BOOK OF COMMON PRAYER*

The Lord keeps watch over his children and comforts those who are waiting for that eternal embrace with him.

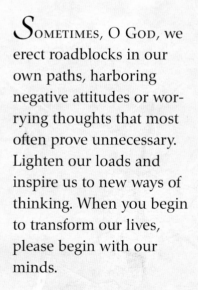

For as he thinketh in his heart, so is he.
PROVERBS 23:7, KJV

*S*OMETIMES, O GOD, we erect roadblocks in our own paths, harboring negative attitudes or worrying thoughts that most often prove unnecessary. Lighten our loads and inspire us to new ways of thinking. When you begin to transform our lives, please begin with our minds.

July 16

But I trust in you, O Lord; I say, "You are my God." My times are in your hand.
PSALM 31:14–15

MY TIMES ARE IN Thy hand;
   My God, I wish them there;
My life, my friends, my soul I leave
   Entirely to Thy care.
               —WILLIAM F. LLOYD

**Held in the palm of God's hand–
not manipulated by that hand,
not crushed by it, not entrapped
within, but held tenderly with
love, we find our safest place.**

*For what can be known about God is
plain. . . . Ever since the creation of
the world his eternal power and
divine nature, invisible though they
are, have been understood and seen
through the things he has made.*

ROMANS 1:19–20

$\mathcal{G}$OD, I thrill at the thought of you. I know
some say you are just a creation of my imagination, but I know better. The order of this
universe defies mere chance, and I am not
ashamed to say I believe your existence is
undeniable and that you made the entire
world. I praise you today because you are God.

July 18

Those who are attentive to a matter will prosper, and
happy are those who trust in the Lord.

PROVERBS 16:20

LORD, while I go about my
business today, help me to
avoid self-preoccupation
and to notice what is happening around me. Help me
to care enough about my
loved ones, my coworkers,
and my world—to be aware
of what they are up to, how
they are feeling, and how I
can be a good friend.

What is desirable in a person is loyalty.
PROVERBS 19:22

*I*T'S DIFFICULT, Lord, to give people the opportunity to prove themselves. The possibility that they might let me down is always at the back of my mind. But you allow me the chance to succeed or fail each day. You give me a clean slate and then permit me to choose how I will fill it. Therefore, help me also believe the best about others, and grant me the grace to anticipate good things from them. Amen.

Trust men and they will be true to you; treat them greatly and they will show themselves great.

—RALPH WALDO EMERSON

July 20

Beloved, I pray that all may go well with you and that you may be in good health, just as it is well with your soul.

3 JOHN 2

GOD, my body is so amazing! It may have its problems, but even so, it has incredible capabilities. Thank you for all that is right with my body. Thank you that it houses my being and gives me the ability to exist and find meaning in life. Grant me health, heavenly Father, but if I cannot always be healthy, grant me grace to do the best I can and be grateful for all the ways in which my body is a blessing. Help me honor your gift of my body by treating it with appropriate respect.

We can practice kindness toward our body by physically taking care of it and by refraining from negative self-talk, concentrating instead on how well it serves us. And we can extend that kindness to our friends. When we hear them complaining about their looks, we can gently and lovingly express our appreciation for their physical incarnation and our desire for them to treat their body with compassion.

—*THE PRACTICE OF KINDNESS*

July 21

Finally, be strong in the Lord and in the strength of his power.
EPHESIANS 6:10

I DON'T WANT TO BE WEAK, fickle, and uncertain, God. I want to be a person who is solid, knows what is true, and operates with a sense of confidence in you. Where I am weak, Lord, please be my strength. Where I am insecure, teach me to believe in your ability to lead me. Where I am unsteady, please bring your stability to me. Let my life be a testimony to your power.

Be as a tower, firmly set;
Shakes not its top for any blast that blows.
—DANTE

July 22

*O Lord, our Sovereign, how majestic is your name in all
the earth!... what are human beings that you are mindful
of them, mortals that you care for them? Yet you have...
crowned them with glory and honor.*

PSALM 8:1, 4–5

FATHER, when I consider Your
power, the ultimate power, the
only power . . . and when I see
your power focused on my concern . . . I can only watch expec-
tantly for how You will do Your
work in Your way in Your time.
—JENNIFER KENNEDY DEAN, *POWER PRAYING*

**To have the personal attention of God can be
disconcerting until one realizes that his gaze is
tender and full of love and compassion.**

July 23

Remind them to be subject to rulers and authorities, to be obedient, to be ready for every good work, to speak evil of no one, to avoid quarreling, to be gentle, and to show every courtesy to everyone.

TITUS 3:1–2

$\mathcal{H}$EAVENLY FATHER, your son, Jesus, could have called down heaven to destroy his enemies when he was on earth, but he didn't. Revenge wasn't his mission. Love was. Help me to submit, as he did, to a path of gentleness in the strength of your love. Amen.

O, it is excellent
**To have a giant's strength; but it is tyrannous
To use it like a giant.**

—SHAKESPEARE, MEASURE FOR MEASURE

July 24

O Lord, in the morning you hear my voice;…Lead me, O Lord, in your righteousness…; make your way straight before me.
PSALM 5:3, 8

DEAR FATHER GOD,

I acknowledge my need and desire to have an increased spiritual ambition to go deeper in prayer for others. I want to have a greater burden for lost souls. I want to be more sensitized to the promptings of the Holy Spirit when praying for others, and to be more fully obedient to Him.

I am willing to adjust my priorities to have more time with You so that I can have an increased understanding from Your Word of Your character and Your ways.

I now commit to do my part, and I submit to You in faith that You will work these things in and through me. Thank You that You will.

In Jesus' name, Amen.

—JOY DAWSON, INTERCESSION

July 25 🐚

[Love] bears all things, believes all things, hopes all things, endures all things.

1 CORINTHIANS 13:7

*T*HOSE PEOPLE WHO ARE unlikable to me, Lord, are not worthless, though I'm tempted to believe my self-centered thoughts about them. Rather, Lord, these people are precious works of beauty, created by you. And if I bother to look beyond my first impressions, I will be delighted by what I see of you in them.

A weed is no more than a flower in disguise,
Which is seen through at once, if love give a man eyes.
—J. R. LOWELL, *A FABLE FOR CRITICS*

July 26

Blessed are the merciful, for they will receive mercy.

MATTHEW 5:7

*D*EAR GOD, I NEED to see people as you see them. I need to feel compassion in the same way you have compassion for them. Help me to be far more aware of the hurts and sorrows of others and to show them mercy so I might be the instrument of your compassion. This I pray. Amen.

Mercy is humanity's most needed embrace. If the world is to become a better place, we must demonstrate the same mercy God has shown us.

July 27 ●

Whoever is kind to the poor lends to the Lord, and will be repaid in full.

PROVERBS 19:17

$\mathcal{A}$S YOU BLESS ME with prosperity, Lord, I want to share these blessings with as many people as I can. Grant me wisdom and discernment to determine how and to whom I might offer some of what you have provided and thereby help them. Keep me from the greed, arrogance, and indifference that would tarnish the beauty of these blessings.

July 28

The gifts he gave were ... for the work of ministry.

EPHESIANS 4:11–12

*H*ELP ME, GOD, to see that you gave your love in such a way that even the most wicked person can repent and find new life in your grace and mercy, indeed, that your love calls even the worst sinners to become your children. You created each person with a specific purpose to serve in this world. Help me, Lord, to pray that each person will turn away from evil, turn to you, and become your devoted servant. Amen.

**If the world seems cold,
kindle fires to warm it!**

—LUCY LARCOM

July 29

It is not good to eat much honey, or to seek honor on top of honor. Like a city breached, without walls, is one who lacks self-control.

PROVERBS 25:27–28

LORD, TEACH ME to refrain from overindulgence of any kind. I don't want to have any gaping holes of unrestraint in my character, and yet I find myself vulnerable in some areas of life. Forgive my failings regardless of how recent they may be, and help me not to dwell on them. I will embrace this day with a fresh opportunity to live free of excesses while focusing on you.

Gourmets claim that the true enjoyment of fine cuisine requires that you stop just when you would like to have a little bit more. In this way, the connoisseur maintains his interest. Everywhere, knowing how to stop short of satiety helps you savor life and, more important, helps you be free.

—EKNATH EASWARAN

July 30

[Children] are indeed a heritage from the Lord.
PSALM 127:3

OH, HEAVENLY FATHER, how good you are to grant us those first wonderful years we have with our children: the years of first words, first steps, and first days of school. The dimpled cheeks and winsome smiles remain framed in our memory long after our children have grown into adults. What a joy to have these little ones in our lives! Thank you for each precious day with them. Amen.

The teaching of the wise is a foundation of life, so that one may avoid the snares of death.

PROVERBS 13:14

I SEEK YOUR WISDOM, God, in the sound counsel of the mentors you've given me. I value my friends who speak truth to me and aren't afraid to redirect me with their wise counsel. Thank you for giving me your help in this tangible way. Help me never to be too arrogant or too self-sufficient to receive what you have to give me through my friends.

A signpost, like a peer, only warns you about the road ahead. But a map, like a mentor, can show you how to get where you want to go.

—BRUCE BICKEL AND STAN JANTZ, *GOD IS IN THE SMALL STUFF*

My prayer life:

_____

_____

_____

_____

_____

_____

_____

_____

_____

_____

_____

_____

I will walk with integrity of heart
within my house; I will not set before
my eyes anything that is base.

PSALM 101:2–3

HEAVENLY FATHER, despite all the temptations around me, I want to display your holiness to the world. Please protect me from base desires and guard me from evil attitudes. Most of all, shield me from pride so that I will walk humbly before you. Amen.

With our exposure to today's media—a media that indiscriminately portrays unrestrained spending, unrestrained eating, and unrestrained sex—it can be difficult to nurture healthy thoughts, actions, and habits. But as we take responsibility for and control of what goes into our hearts and minds, we quickly discover that it becomes far easier to make good decisions.

August 2

If your eye is pure, there will be sunshine in your soul. But if your eye is clouded with evil thoughts and desires, you are in deep spiritual darkness. And oh, how deep that darkness can be!

MATTHEW 6:22–23 TLB

*L*ORD GOD, I want to be honest and genuine. Set me free from the pride and fear that get in the way of truthfulness. It's refreshing to meet other people who are being themselves and not putting on a false persona. I want to always be that kind of person—a breath of fresh air that allows others to be themselves as well.

The face is the part of the human body which most surely reveals character and mood. It is essentially the part of our bodies which is to be looked at....To be able to look a person in the face is to be fairly and squarely on genuine, honest terms with that person.

—HARRY BALMIRES

August 3

Every word of God proves true; he is a shield to those who take refuge in him.

PROVERBS 30:5

I'VE COME TO REALIZE, dear Lord, that while truth is the best path, it can also be a difficult one. I don't always want to hear or face the truth. It usually means making some changes, and transitions are usually uncomfortable. But, God, to continue living lies is absurd once the truth has been made clear. So as I move toward a life of honesty and authenticity, please keep nurturing within my soul a longing for what is true.

God offers to every mind its choice between truth and repose.

—EMERSON, *ESSAYS*

August 4

*Jesus said to him, "I am the way, and
the truth, and the life."*

JOHN 14:6

LORD, YOU SHED YOUR LIGHT of truth within
our hearts and minds. You bring understanding where there is confusion. You bring
certainty where there is doubt. You fill our
hearts with hope where there was once
despair. Thank you for the ability to per-
ceive your light and to walk in the freedom
of truth. Help us not only to embrace you as
the light of our lives, but also to proclaim
you as the light of the world.

**We don't need to employ contemporary jargon in order to
bring enlightenment. Enlightenment came when Jesus came!
Enlightenment is here now in His Spirit—more real than the
sunlight flooding my yard and breaking into the woods around
my house....We don't need a new light; we need to begin to act
on the fact of the Light is already with us, around us, and in us
in the presence of Jesus Christ.**

—EUGENIA PRICE

*Look on my right hand and see—there is no one
who takes notice of me; no refuge remains to me; no
one cares for me.… Give heed to my cry, for I am
brought very low.… The righteous will surround
me, for you will deal bountifully with me.*

PSALM 142:4, 6–7

OH, GOD, we go through life so lonely,
needing what other people can give us,
yet ashamed to show that need. And
other people go through life so lonely,
hungering for what it would be such a
joy for us to give. Dear God, please bring
us together, the people who need each
other, who can help each other, and
would so enjoy each other.

—MARJORIE HOLMES, *I'VE GOT TO TALK TO SOMEBODY, GOD*

**Allow yourself to receive help from someone
today, whether it is allowing someone to open
a door for you or accepting someone's offer to
assist you with an overwhelming task. Then
ask God to present you with someone you can
help. You will be blessed on both counts!**

August 6

Make no friends with those given to anger, and do not associate with hotheads, or you may learn their ways and entangle yourself in a snare.

PROVERBS 22:24–25

$\mathcal{H}$EAVENLY FATHER, HELP ME take stock of the influences in my life. Are there any friendships that are getting in the way of my commitment to honor you? Are there any relationships in which I need to step up and be more truthful about my values and convictions, rather than just following along and feeling pangs of regret later? Are there people who nurture my soul with whom I could be spending more time? I don't want my relationship with you to slip into some cold, lost place because I have not been careful to keep good company. Give me courage and strength today to be faithful to you, my dearest of all friends. Amen.

It's easier to change your behavior in advance than to change your reputation afterward.
—BRUCE BICKEL AND STAN JANTZ, *GOD IS IN THE SMALL STUFF*

Therefore, do not let sin exercise dominion in your mortal bodies, to make you obey their passions.... For sin will have no dominion over you, since you are not under law but under grace.

ROMANS 6:12, 14

*L*ORD, THANK YOU for the interests, convictions, and loves that help drive me toward meaningful action. But, God, I need your wisdom to keep watch over my natural passions. I can sometimes become obsessed or act compulsively, speak out of turn, or not know when to stop pushing myself and others. Forgive the times I've gotten carried away, and help me learn from those mistakes. Please work through my mind to steer my heart in good and healthy directions.

It is with our passions, as it is with fire and water, they are good servants but bad masters.
—SIR ROGER L'ESTRANGE

August 8

I will give thanks to the Lord with my whole heart; I will tell of all your wonderful deeds. I will be glad and exult in you; I will sing praise to your name, O Most High.

PSALM 9:1–2

I AM HAPPY because you have accepted me, dear Lord.
Sometimes I do not know what to do with all my
    happiness.
I swim in your grace like a whale in the ocean.
The saying goes: "An ocean never dries up,"
but we know that your grace also never fails.
Dear Lord, your grace is our happiness. Hallelujah!

—PRAYER FROM WEST AFRICA

**Praise flows constantly from
the wellspring of love created
in one's heart by God's grace.**

August 9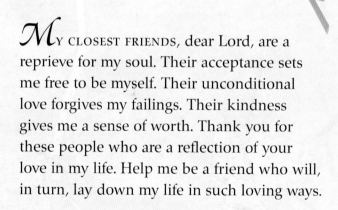

*This is my commandment, that you love
one another as I have loved you. No one
has greater love than this, to lay down
one's life for one's friends.*

JOHN 15:12–13

$\mathcal{M}$Y CLOSEST FRIENDS, dear Lord, are a
reprieve for my soul. Their acceptance sets
me free to be myself. Their unconditional
love forgives my failings. Their kindness
gives me a sense of worth. Thank you for
these people who are a reflection of your
love in my life. Help me be a friend who will,
in turn, lay down my life in such loving ways.

August 10

The Lord our God spoke to us at Horeb, saying, "You have stayed long enough at this mountain."

DEUTERONOMY 1:6

IT'S TIME, LORD, for a change. Time to move forward and leave the ruts behind. Pull me, push me, and lift me—whatever it takes! Just don't let me stay here and become a fixture in the halls of an unchallenging existence. I need to be stretched and bent and moved so I can continue to grow. There are physical therapists who help people increase their range of physical motion and ability. God, be my spiritual therapist! Take my spirit to new levels of strength and movement. I am ready to follow your instructions.

August 11

Do not be afraid of sudden panic, or of the storm that strikes... for the Lord will be your confidence and will keep your foot from being caught.

PROVERBS 3:25–26

O LORD, I FEEL my heart panic from those forces that seem to overwhelm me. I am so afraid, because my world seems to be in such horrible jeopardy. Help me, O Lord, to turn to you for courage during this dreadful time. Increase my faith and strengthen my confidence in your care for my welfare. This, I pray. Amen.

In what do you believe today despite your circumstances? In whom do you trust today, given your circumstances? Let faith be your resting place–your sanctuary in the middle of chaos.

August 12

But for me it is good to be near God; I have made the Lord God my refuge, to tell of all your works.

PSALM 73:28

O BLESSED SAVIOUR, draw us; draw us by the chords of thy love; draw us by the sense of thy goodness; draw us by thyself; draw us by the unspotted purity and beauty of thy example; draw us by the merit of thy precious death and by the power of thy Holy Spirit; draw us, good Lord, and we shall run after thee. Amen.

—ISAAC BARROW

Feeling near to God gives me the sense of being exactly where I belong.

Let us run with perseverance the race that is set before us,
looking to Jesus the pioneer and perfecter of our faith,
who for the sake of the joy that was set before him endured
the cross, disregarding its shame, and has taken his seat
at the right hand of the throne of God.

HEBREWS 12:1–2

I BELIEVE IN YOU, God. I believe you are
the peace that conquers my most pressing
problem, the sufficiency that meets my
greatest need, and the strength that is
equal to my most difficult task. There's
nothing that is too much for me when I'm
trusting you. Forgive me for the moments
when I lose sight of these realities and
lapse into worry or fear or pride. But
whenever I refocus on you—on who you
are—I see through eyes of faith again, and
you heal my perspective once more.

August 14

Jesus said, "I give you a new commandment, that you love one another. Just as I have loved you, you also should love one another. By this everyone will know that you are my disciples, if you have love for one another."

JOHN 13:34–35

O GOD, YOUR LOVE IS so great. I'm not sure that I can love as you do or even love others in a way that will please you. God, teach me how to really love my family, my friends, and even strangers. I trust in the power of your love to make me into a far more loving person than I am today. Amen.

When God's love is seen in my relationships with friends and family, the world gets a glimpse of God's saving grace.

August 15

Love is patient; love is kind; . . . It does not insist on its own way.
1 CORINTHIANS 13:4–5

IF ONLY I COULD HELP them, God. Sometimes I just wish I could reach into their lives and change them—to save them the struggle and pain of learning the hard way. But, Lord, that's not your plan, and I need to be willing to wait as you work gently from the inside out in the lives of those I love. Help me to not say too much. Help me to not say too little. Grant me wisdom and sensitivity in my words, and most of all, help me not to be afraid to say, "I love you."

Letting other people grow, develop, live their own experiences as they must takes courage and acceptance of the knowledge that our responsibility in this life is to our own healthy development—not to controlling someone else's.

—KAREN CASEY AND MARTHA VANCEBURG, *THE PROMISE OF A NEW DAY*

August 16

And the king will answer them, "Truly I tell you, just as you did it to one of the least of these who are members of my family, you did it to me."

MATTHEW 25:40

I<small>N THIS SEASON</small> of picnics and vacations, God, guide us to look around for ways to share our bounty so that all can feast. Indeed, our cups over-flow, and there is more than enough to go around.

Action may not always bring happiness, but there is no happiness without action.

August 17

The apostle Paul wrote to his apprentice Timothy, "You then, my child, be strong in the grace that is in Christ Jesus; and what you have heard from me through many witnesses entrust to faithful people who will be able to teach others as well."

2 TIMOTHY 2:1–2

LORD, THERE ARE THOSE you have placed into my life who look to me for leadership. They take cues for their lives from mine. What a great privilege and a sobering responsibility it is! Help me lead with integrity and love. Let your truth be the hallmark of my choices and words, and let your mercy and grace characterize my attitudes and actions. And when all is said and done, heavenly Father, may those you have given me to lead ultimately become more like you. Amen.

August 18

Jesus said, "Take care that you do not despise one of these little ones; for, I tell you, in heaven their angels continually see the face of my Father in heaven.... So it is not the will of your Father in heaven that one of these little ones should be lost."

MATTHEW 18:10, 14

LORD, I PRAY for these children. Show them what is right and wrong and how to be a true child of yours. I pray that each one will discover your love and abide in your grace. Amen.

The children are watching us more closely than we know. We nurture or destroy their sense of right and wrong, depending on how we respond to our own conscience. As we make choices today, we should stop and ask ourselves, *How will this affect the young hearts and minds that depend on me for guidance?*

*And now faith, hope, and love abide, these
three; and the greatest of these is love.*
1 CORINTHIANS 13:13

MY HEAVENLY FATHER, whose love is perfect, what do I
have to fear when you are the one caring for me? And
yet, I do fear; irrationally I fear, despite your faithfulness,
despite your assurances, and despite your promises.
Why do I still fear? I don't always understand my trem-
bling heart and the shadows of things far smaller
than you before which it cowers. Please liberate
me from these lapses of trust. Free me to stand
fearlessly, supported by faith and hope, in the
center of your great love for me.

To let go is to fear less and love more.
—AUTHOR UNKNOWN

# August 20

*In all toil there is profit, but mere
talk leads only to poverty.*

PROVERBS 14:23

SOMETIMES, LORD, I feel as if my life is a lot of busywork with no real direction and no significant contribution to the larger good. Help me, heavenly Father, to see the meaning in the tasks you've given me to do, and if I am spending my time and energy poorly, please redirect my efforts. Maximize the strengths, gifts, and talents you've given me so I can experience the fulfillment in my work that you intend. May your plans be accomplished and your name and reputation be enhanced because of how you work through my life.

**Develop a cause for your life.
Whatever it is, dedicate
yourself to it daily.**
—BRUCE BICKEL AND STAN JANTZ,
GOD IS IN THE SMALL STUFF

August 21

Happy are those to whom the Lord imputes no iniquity, and in whose spirit there is no deceit.... I acknowledged my sin to you, and I did not hide my iniquity; I said, "I will confess my transgressions to the Lord," and you forgave the guilt of my sin.

PSALM 32:2, 5

My HEAVENLY FATHER, I have stumbled again. I am so sorry that I have turned away from your will and did what I knew was not right and holy. Please forgive me. Please extend your grace to me once more. O God, I know you love me and are ready to welcome me back into your arms. Thank you for your mercy. Amen.

There is no relief so sweet as the relief of coming clean to God and living again in the truth.

August 22

So then, brothers and sisters, we are debtors, not to the flesh, to live according to the flesh—for if you live according to the flesh, you will die; but if by the Spirit you put to death the deeds of the body, you will live.

ROMANS 8:12–13

God, I want to live fully and passionately. I don't want to miss a thing. And I'm persuaded that I can live with abandon—to seize the day—without being reckless and foolish. Help me make the most of every opportunity you give me, and grant me the physical, mental, and emotional stamina to enjoy each day. Keep me from overindulgence that might put any aspect of my life out of balance. And if I do start slipping into some unhealthy habits, God, please make me aware of the danger, and grant me the grace to respond to your warnings. I love you. I love the life you've given me. Let it be filled with all the wonder you've intended for me from the beginning. Amen.

For the Lord God is a sun and a shield; he bestows favor and honor. No good thing does the Lord withhold from those who walk uprightly.

PSALM 84:11

*W*E THANK YOU, God, for the moments of fulfillment:
the end of a day's work,
the harvest of sugarcane,
the birth of a child,
for in these pauses we feel the rhythm of the eternal.

—PRAYER FROM HAWAII

There is glory in the ordinary, satisfaction in the simple. Find it today and let wonder and praise fill your soul.

August 24

Run in such a way that you may win... Athletes exercise self-control in all things; they do it to receive a perishable wreath, but we an imperishable one.

1 CORINTHIANS 9:24–25

HEAVENLY FATHER, sometimes I'm my own worst enemy. I sabotage your efforts to bring victory to my life. Please forgive me for the times I've resisted you. Help me look ahead to my eternal rest with you to remind me why I'm here now. Bring your blessing of self-discipline to my life, for, ironically, it is in disciplining myself that I find freedom and victory over life-eroding habits such as apathy and laziness. Yes, God, I know there is freedom when I give myself happily and fully to your purposes.

*But you will receive power when the Holy
Spirit has come upon you; and you will be
my witnesses . . . to the ends of the earth.*

ACTS 1:8

*H*OLY SPIRIT:
As the wind is your symbol, so forward our goings.
As the dove so launch us heavenwards.
As water, so purify our spirits.
As a cloud so abate our temptations.
As dew so revive our languor.
As fire so purge out our dross.

—CHRISTINA ROSSETTI

**God's Spirit empowers us to
do and be what we could
never do and be by our own
initiative or in our own power.**

August 26

I lie down and sleep; I wake again, for the Lord sustains me.

PSALM 3:5

WHEN I WAS A CHILD, heavenly Father, I would kneel at bedtime and pray, "Now I lay me down to sleep, I pray the Lord my soul to keep..." It's been a long time since those evenings when I'd offer my petitions to you. I must say you've always been faithful to me and kept me in your care. Over the years, as I've grown older, there have been nighttimes of the soul that have darkened my mood and per-spective. Yet, you have never left me alone. No, you have stayed close by me until daybreak. Even now you are with me. I know it beyond a doubt.

August 27

Day by day, . . . they broke bread at home and ate their food with glad and generous hearts, praising God.

ACTS 2:46–47

TO GOD WHO GIVES our daily bread
A thankful song we raise,
And pray that he who sends us food
May fill our hearts with praise.

—THOMAS TALLIS

Mealtimes are ideal times for pausing to consider all the gifts God gives us and also to think of ways we might give away some of those blessings.

August 28

Give instruction to the wise, and they will become wiser still;
teach the righteous and they will gain in learning.

PROVERBS 9:9

I'M READY TO LEARN something new today, Lord. I know from experience that some lessons are pleasant, while others can be painful. But it seems that as I grow in wisdom, the understanding from lessons learned in the past makes my way smoother. Thank you for that growth process. Keep me in it, I pray, and grant me grace today to accept your instruction through the people and circumstances I encounter.

I'll remember: Today I'm a student and my experiences are my teachers.

—KAREN CASEY AND MARTHA
VANCEBURG, *THE PROMISE OF A NEW DAY*

Thus says the Lord: Stand at the crossroads, and look, and ask for the ancient paths, where the good way lies; and walk in it, and find rest for your souls.

JEREMIAH 6:16

My DEAR LORD, you are my resting place. This world has wearied my soul, but you are here for me so that I may regain my strength and desire to move on. I lean on you, and your arms uplift me. Thank you for this rest. Amen.

The way to rest is often some road back to a place in our past, a place we have mistakenly forgotten, a place to which we need to return.

August 30

I believe that I shall see the goodness of the Lord in the land of the living. Wait for the Lord; be strong, and let your heart take courage; wait for the Lord!

PSALM 27:13–14

THERE ARE TIMES WHEN death seems like an attractive alternative to having to face certain things in this world. Lord, I don't mean to be ungrateful for my life when I say that, but I am crying out for your help and for a new measure of strength from you in order to press on. You know my limitations and my vulnerabilities when life gets ugly. I know them, too. There are no secrets between us, and for that I am thankful. I can come to you without pretense. So today, it's just me standing here, open and honest before you, longing for your help. I know you will give it freely in just the right way and at just the right time. I trust you. Let me live boldly with the courage you lend me today. Amen.

For a day in your courts is better than a thousand elsewhere. I would rather be a doorkeeper in the house of my God than live in the tents of wickedness.

PSALM 84:10

I LOVE YOU, O my God, and my only desire is to love you until the last breath of my life. I love you, and I would rather die loving you, than live without loving you. I love you, Lord, and the only grace I ask is to love you eternally. My God, if my tongue cannot say in every moment that I love you, I want my heart to repeat this to you as often as I draw breath.

—JEAN-BAPTISTE MARIE VIANNEY

God made us for love. He longs to hear our authentic expressions of love for him. How will you tell God that you love him today? What will you do? What will you say?

My prayer life:

_____

_____

_____

_____

_____

_____

_____

_____

_____

_____

_____

_____

_____

September 1

Then Jesus went about all the cities and villages, teaching in their synagogues, and proclaiming the good news of the kingdom, and curing every disease and every sickness. When he saw the crowds, he had compassion for them.... Then he said to his disciples, "The harvest is plentiful, but the laborers are few; therefore ask the Lord of the harvest to send out laborers into his harvest."

MATTHEW 9:35–38

JESUS, YOU SAW the value of people. You loved people and reached out to them with compassion and healing. You saw men, women, and children in vast numbers, coming to you for help, and you compared them to a harvest field, ripe for salvation. O Jesus! You have reaped my soul into your kingdom. Change me into one who harvests and use my life to gather others into your eternal love.

If your vision is for a year, plant wheat. If your vision is for ten years, plant trees. If your vision is for a lifetime, plant people.

—CHINESE PROVERB

September 2

> *O Lord, my heart is not lifted up, my eyes are not raised too high;... But I have calmed and quieted my soul, like a weaned child with its mother; my soul is like the weaned child that is with me.*
>
> PSALM 131:1–2

*P*LEASE MAKE OF MY LIFE what You would have it be. Time and fate have twisted things I cannot straighten out alone. Dear God, may I begin again. My body, my mind, my spirit, my love, my hate, my pain, my sorrows, my joy, my questions, my fears, my hopes, my visions, I give them all to You. Amen.

—MARIANNE WILLIAMSON

When the quiet after the storm finally comes to our hearts, we look up to find that God is still with us, holding us close to his heart.

September 3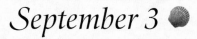

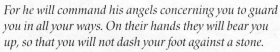

For he will command his angels concerning you to guard
you in all your ways. On their hands they will bear you
up, so that you will not dash your foot against a stone.
PSALM 91:11–12

OH LORD, WE GIVE YOU thanks for your presence,
which greets us each day in the guise of a friend, a work
of nature, or a story from a stranger. In our times of
deepest need, we are reminded through these messen-
gers that you are indeed watching over us. God, I have
known you in the love and care of a friend, which
envelopes me and keeps me company in my despair.
When I observe the last morning glory stretching faithfully to receive what warmth is left in today's chilly sunshine, I am heartened and inspired to do the same.
When I am hesitant to speak up and then read in the
newspaper a story of courage in controversy, I find my
voice lifted and strengthened by your message in black-
and-white type. For all the angelic messages that surround us every day, God, we are grateful receivers.

Let us not be justices of the
peace, but angels of peace.
—ST. THERESA OF LISIEUX

September 4

You must follow exactly the path that the Lord your God has commanded you, so that you may live, and that it may go well with you, and that you may live long in the land that you are to possess.

DEUTERONOMY 5:33

GOD, I WANT TO FOLLOW your path for me, but I'm overwhelmed. There are so many needs and demands surrounding me. Your creation remains an unfinished work, and I feel too small and inadequate to partner with you. I'm tired of striving to faithfully be your loving arms and responsive footsteps to those who are in need. When I have lost my path, remind me to trace Christ's steps. Jesus gave what food he had, and you multiplied it; gave what comfort he could, and you blessed it; spoke of the good news to those he met, and through your Spirit it continues to spread like goldenrod through a meadow. Keep me focused, God, on the path before me, even when it seems stacked with insurmountable obstacles. Remind me that I do not walk alone, but with all those whose aim is to walk with you.

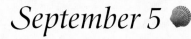

September 5

He is the reflection of God's glory and the
exact imprint of God's very being, and he
sustains all things by his powerful word.
HEBREWS 1:3

$\mathcal{G}$OD, YOU BLESS US with the gift of perseverance that
keeps us upright in the face of all that threatens to topple
us. You bless us with the gift of hope, which sustains our
energy while we work to make real that which we are
hoping for. You bless us with the gift of love, which
buffers our hearts from all that could break them. You
bless us with the gift of compassion, which
enables us to shoulder one another's burdens
and celebrate one another's joys. For your sus-
taining power, we offer our praise.

**Faith is for that which lies on the other
side of reason. Faith is what makes life
bearable, with all its tragedies and
ambiguities and sudden, startling joys.**
—MADELEINE L'ENGLE, *GLIMPSES OF GRACE*

September 6

When they saw that the star had stopped,
they were overwhelmed with joy.
MATTHEW 2:10

LONG AGO, GOD, to
those scanning a night sky,
you sent a star. To those
tending sheep on a silent
hill, you sent an angel
chorus. What sign will you
send me to be and do all I
can? Let me hear, see, and
accept it when it arrives.

**Happiness is a butterfly, which, when pursued
is always just beyond your grasp, but which, if
you will sit quietly, may alight upon you.**
—NATHANIEL HAWTHORNE

September 7

*They shall beat their swords into plowshares, and their
spears into pruning hooks; nation shall not lift up sword
against nation, neither shall they learn war any more.*

ISAIAH 2:4

*T*ODAY, GOD, I ponder past battles when
world conflict took the lives of millions of
men, women, and children. Even now lives
are being lost because of war. I try to make
room for peace in my heart, for I am one of
your squabbling children. May lion-with-
lamb peace sprout first within me and then
overflow onto others, inspired by the love
you've sent into this world. Amen.

**Peace is not the absence of
conflict, but the handling of
conflict without loss of balance.**

—RABBI RAMI M. SHAPIRO,
HEAL YOUR SOUL, HEAL THE WORLD

September 8

He will yet fill your mouth with laughter,
and your lips with shouts of joy.

JOB 8:21

*S*PILLS, SPLATTERS, and blunders punctuate my daily life, Lord. Before lamenting or scolding, I try to take a cue from babies—giggles are on their lips long before words. Instead of berating myself for my mistakes and shortcomings, help me experience the joy that comes with being accepted just as I am, thankful for the ability to laugh at myself, knowing you are smiling beside us.

If you're not allowed to laugh in
heaven, I don't want to go there.
—MARTIN LUTHER

September 9

And all of us, with unveiled faces, seeing the glory of the Lord as though reflected in a mirror, are being transformed into the same image from one degree of glory to another; for this comes from the Lord, the Spirit.

2 CORINTHIANS 3:18

WE'RE NOT PERFECT, Father, but we are yours. We're not what we should be, but we do claim your salvation and your grace. We ask you to make us every day more and more into the image of Jesus Christ. We stand amazed that you would have such mercy upon us to forgive us time and time again. Thank you for the immeasurable depth of your grace.

—*THE INSPIRATIONAL STUDY BIBLE*

When we are alone in our most honest moments, we long to be better people. Only God can transform us and make us more like Jesus.

September 10

Jesus said, "I am the vine, you are the branches. Those who abide in me and I in them bear much fruit, because apart from me you can do nothing."

JOHN 15:5

*G*OD, YOU ARE THE SOURCE of life. I confess that at times I have sought to disconnect from your Spirit and pull away from your presence. I have pretended to be ripened and completed fruit, no longer in need of its home on the vine. In reality, though, I continue to develop and ripen. As long as I live, I am like seeds, blossoms, and green fruit. Hold onto me, Vine of Life, that I may grow in your sustenance, becoming more and more all that you desire me to become.

Vintners excel at grafting—that is, joining of branches to the sturdy prime vine so the best fruit can grow to fullest bouquet. Some grafts don't take, falling aside. Within moments, they begin to shrivel, removed from the root that offers new life and nourishment.

September 11 🐚

CONFUSION IS DIRECTING my thoughts
like a drunken general ineffectively
attempting to marshal his troops. My
mind loyally follows its erratic demands
and becomes increasingly lost and frustrated. I need a sign, a marker, something
to orient myself, to find my way out of
this turmoil. Find me, Lord, for I am wandering in the wilderness of my own mind,
heading deeper and deeper into despair.
"Where are you?" I call. And then I realize
that as I describe my lostness, you show
me where I am and how to return home.

September 12

Be angry but do not sin.
EPHESIANS 4:26

MERCIFUL GOD, I need to borrow some of your compassion because I have no mercy in my heart at this moment. Punishment would be great just about now, nothing overboard, just give them what they deserve. And yet, in the silence I seem to hear you ask, "And what would that be?" My anger fills in possibilities like scenes from a television pilot. Which plot, which vengeance will release my rage? What kind of ending would represent your will? But, God, I know what you are really asking. Please take my anger and transform it into mercy—the mercy you have shown me.

God hears and receives our anger, for it's sometimes all the prayer we have. Its heat is a fiery furnace consuming in the darkness, but God refines that passion and transforms it into a new life.

September 13

Jesus declared, "The Spirit of the Lord is upon me,…
he hath sent me to heal the broken-hearted."

LUKE 4:18, KJV

I AM LIKE TWO HALVES of a walnut, God. I am of two minds: despairing and hopeful. Help me feel your hand holding me together as I rebuild my life when at first it seemed too hard to try. In order to get to the meat of a walnut, it must be split into halves. May the brokenness I feel get me to the meat, the nourishment I need in order to move on. Amen.

September 14

*G*OD, THE WIND HAS BEEN blowing so hard for so long. How much longer must I stay curled up in a ball behind this large stone, seeking protection from the storm that swirls around me? I have watched the weeds bow and bend and still not break against the onslaught of the wind and the rain. God, I sense I must seek to bend and bow in the midst of the strong forces that pummel me. In bending, I will not break, and I will find new strength to endure until the morning light comes when you will help me to stand once again.

The little reed, bending to the force of the wind, soon stood upright again when the storm had passed over.

—AESOP

September 15

For in hope we were saved. Now hope that is seen is not hope. For who hopes for what is seen? But if we hope for what we do not see, we wait for it with patience.
ROMANS 8:24–25

I REJOICE TODAY, GOD, because I finally figured it out! I've been practicing and practicing and not once did I get it right. Every day I've been working with no evidence of progress. In fact, last week I was sure I had made things worse, repeating the same mistakes. And then this morning, it clicked, it flowed, it worked! Thank you for helping me persevere and for the encouragement of teachers and loved ones, who tolerated my whining and frustrated efforts. Help me learn from this moment that frustration does not mean failure; success is always just underneath the surface.

To believe what is unseen, like a cinder hiking trail hidden beneath the snow, reaps the reward of seeing what we believe.

September 16

When the cares of my heart are many,
your consolations cheer my soul.

PSALM 94:19

I'M OFTEN TOO PROUD to seek or accept advice, God. Like a two-year-old with a turtleneck, I'd rather get my head stuck doing it myself than accept assistance. Thank you for circumventing my stubbornness today, showering me with possibilities like seeds scattered on a rain-soaked garden. Thank you for your help, which comes in many ways and forms. God, I'm so grateful.

Faith teaches a new math, which subtracts old ways and adds new thoughts, for sharing with God divides troubles and multiplies possibilities.

September 17

To you they cried, and were saved; in you they trusted.

PSALM 22:5

THE SYMPTOMS DID NOT signal what we all had feared. God, I was so scared. Yet, I could tell by the doctor's footsteps approaching the door that they were coming to bring me good news, and her opening smile confirmed that the waiting was over and had not been in vain. Use my fear, God, that it may become energy to live more fully, with more appreciation, from this day on.

Close calls to body, mind, and soul remind us to live each day as a newfound treasure.

September 18

God, the Lord, is my strength.
HABAKKUK 3:19

GOD, I HOLD FAST to you at this present
moment, for it is the only way for me to have
perspective and hope for life beyond this
pain I have. And yet, come quickly for I am
tired. Fill me with your strength for I feel
weak. Add meaning to these days of pain and
finally call me to a new day when I can serve
you with renewed purpose and passion.

**After trouble recedes, remind
me to continue to pray, even
when life becomes peaceful
again. Please, Lord, teach me
to laugh again but don't ever
let me forget that I cried.**

September 19

I'M COUNTING THREE SOCKS, two plastic
heroes, and an empty juice box. It's been
a peaceful evening, dear God. Everyone is
in a good mood, and it's almost bedtime.
I could pick this stuff up in 30 seconds
and lecture her tomorrow, or I can tell her
to pick up her mess, risking tears, resist-
ance, and an end to the harmony. I'm
tired too, did I mention that? I really
don't have the energy for a scene. Come
here, sweetie, I hear myself calling. I've
discovered the secret hideout of her
clothes and toys. Thank you, God, for the
gift of humor. Help me use it more often
to augment my discipline.

**Character building begins in our
infancy and continues until death.**
—ELEANOR ROOSEVELT

September 20

*For the mountains may depart and the hills be removed,
but my steadfast love shall not depart from you, and my
covenant of peace shall not be removed, says the Lord,
who has compassion on you.*

ISAIAH 54:10

GOD, I READ THE BILLBOARD protesting the pollution
of our air and water. May my response convey my
commitment to its message—more than simply donat-
ing to good causes. Creator God, have compassion on
us, who continue to destroy this amazing planet we
call home, more out of our love of convenience than
any maliciousness. Forgive us for moving mountains
and hills to make room for strip malls and parking
lots. Thank you for calling us to be good stewards of
this planet you've created and given us. Amen.

**Having faith in God's grace, we
know that he who created this
natural world will neither
abandon it nor us—especially us.**

September 21

We will all be changed.
1 CORINTHIANS 15:51

DO YOUR CHILDREN, like me, ever irritate you, God, when we complain while you have to drag us to a place where we can receive blessings from your hand? For days I whine about having to go here or there. After a crazy, harried week, I just want to stay home and relax in my pajamas; I don't want to get dressed up and make small talk with people I barely know. I did not anticipate the gifts you had for me there. Thank you, Patient Friend, for gifts wrapped in experiences I've tried to reject.

A life in disarray is ripe for a second chance. Yet, how often we seem intent upon missing it. In God's hands, troubles can be disguised invitations into a new life.

September 22

[God] gives breath to the people … and spirit to those who walk in it.

ISAIAH 42:5

*D*ID YOU SEE THAT, God? Her canoe hit that rock and dumped her into the icy rapids, and she's laughing! Chasing after the canoe heading downstream but caught by the guide, she is stumbling and floundering her way through the water. I had no idea she had it in her, not only physically but in her spirit! I've been feeling hungry, tired, and cranky, and I'm still dry and without a bruise. She has embraced her cold, wet, painful fall with exuberance and a spirit of adventure. For this new window into this lovely soul, I am grateful and inspired.

What lies behind us and what lies before us are tiny matters compared to what lies within us.
—AUTHOR UNKNOWN

September 23

O<small>H, SING TO THE</small> L<small>ORD</small> a new song!
I sort of like the old tunes that bring soft
memories to mind and that soothe my
soul with the sounds of days gone by. But
those new songs have a rhythm and a
beat that the kids of today are moving to,
and I must confess, they are very catchy.
God, I pray to stay in touch and in tune
with where your Spirit is luring me, and
all of us, to go. My fear of tomorrow
I relinquish to your love of me today.

**My passport into the future is a lively interest in today's world.
It keeps my mind receptive to newfangled thoughts, gadgets,
and ideas; surely the best way to keep young!**

September 24

Sing to the Lord a new song.
ISAIAH 42:10

$\mathcal{G}$OD, CAN WE TALK? Being childlike is easy for children; they don't know what we adults know can and will happen. But, Lord, I long for the simple honesty of being a child, who lives fully in the warmth of summer sand with outstretched arms mirroring the worship of the trees, waving limbs at the grandeur of the universe. It was fun just remembering. Maybe a few moments of childlikeness won't hurt all that much. Thank you, God.

Pray barefoot today, curling the toes and stretching heavenward. Lived with the heart of a child, each day is a whole-body celebration!

September 25

Send out your bread upon the waters, for after many days you will get it back.

ECCLESIASTES 11:1

GOD, I BELIEVE IN doing good. I believe in sending my good intentions out into the waves of life. But, God, help me in my unbelief, because I'm not sure that I believe that good will really come back to me. Help me not focus on what good should come to me, but remind me what good I need to give out. Help me trust in your goodness and believe that it is in giving that I will receive. Amen.

Even when no one says thank you, reaching beyond yourself to help or touch another comes back to you—it's heard in the heart.

September 26

If anyone strikes you on the cheek, offer the other also.
LUKE 6:29

*L*ORD, WHEN WILL THE hard-blowing wind finally cease? What if it has blown me so totally adrift that I am lost? What if I have turned away from your love? What am I to do? The person who has wronged me has caused such a storm in my life that I feel I am sinking fast into the depths of anger and despair. Please, God, steady my soul and propel me to do what is right—what you want me to do in response.

When someone speaks harshly about or to you, hurting your feelings, just move your sails out of their wind.

September 27

Happy are the people…who walk…in the light of your countenance.

PSALM 89:15

GOD, I GREW UP living around people who were exceedingly stern. But your ways are so much gentler than theirs. Walking in the light of your presence is a joy unequaled in this world. Help me, God, to learn to be gentle and loving while you cast your tender light on me. To be able to just see the light of your countenance is joy enough for me.

Happiness results from putting hearts and minds to work for our Lord and doing it with joy and vigor.

September 28

For by grace you have been saved through faith.
EPHESIANS 2:8

GOD, LET ME BE the first to say that I
have no way to comprehend what it
means that by grace I have been saved
through faith. Forgive me, God. I can be
so dense at times. Is it sufficient that I
accept that you love me, even more than I
can know? Is it enough that I serve the
needs of the world because of your great
love moving in and through me? Is this
faith that I have? It feels as if I have no
other adequate response than to follow
the way of your dear Son.

**Nothing is more wondrous than faith–the one
great moving force which we can neither weigh
in the balance nor test in the crucible.**
—WILLIAM OSLER

September 29

I HESITATE TO QUIET myself in prayer, O Great Listener, because I know that you do hear me. Even before I pray I know so much of what is required of me. To love justice, to do mercy, and to walk humbly with you. Your patience with me is nearly endless. I'm humbled by your great love, which is more than willing and able to lure me toward my completion in this life. In prayer, I'm moved to relinquish my reticence to move ahead in the ways of love. Praise to you, O Great and Wondrous Friend.

Prayer does not change God, but it changes him who prays.
—SØREN KIERKEGAARD

September 30

*By awesome deeds you answer us...you
are the hope of all the ends of the earth.*

PSALM 65:5

GOD, AS I THINK about the many
directions my life has gone, I know I
have usually chosen well-trod paths.
But, here and there, I have gone off on
roads less traveled and have discovered a richness to life unknown to me
before. When I have looked back over
my shoulder, I am sure that it was you
whom I saw passing off into the shadows. You were there, weren't you? You
were there leading me on this road less
traveled. Thank you, God, for always
being present, beckoning me forward
to the goal you've planned for me.
Amen.

My prayer life:

_____

_____

_____

_____

_____

_____

_____

_____

_____

_____

_____

_____

_____

October 1

Then they were glad because they had quiet, and [the Lord] brought them to their desired haven.

PSALM 107:30

IT SEEMS THAT MY summer activities are always more than I anticipate, heavenly Father. I love the vacations, barbecues, and weekend outings, but after a while, I get tired of it all. How welcome the fall is with the beginning of familiar routines and the quiet settling into that pace. Thank you for this time, for the calming sanctuary of autumn, and for my home, where I rediscover the goodness of this season you've given me.

All things on earth point home in old October.
—THOMAS WOLFE, *OF TIME AND THE RIVER*

October 2

May there be abundance of grain in the land; may it wave on the tops of the mountains; may its fruit be like Lebanon; and may people blossom in the cities like the grass of the field.

PSALM 72:16

O GOD, HOW BEAUTIFUL is this season of harvest and change! Autumn celebrates what summer has accomplished: fruit, wheat, vegetables, and even hay for the animals. All of these things are miracles. They grow from tiny seeds in the ground and amazingly spring up and become our sustenance for another year. How do you do it, God? We know the facts, but the miracle still remains. I praise you, gracious Provider, for the wonder of your goodness and love toward us.

> Season of mists and mellow fruitfulness,
> Close bosom-friend of the maturing sun;
> Conspiring with him how to load and bless
> With fruit the vines that round the thatch-eaves run.
>
> —JOHN KEATS, "TO AUTUMN"

October 3

*Blessed are the pure in heart, for
they will see God.*

MATTHEW 5:8

I PRAY THEE, Lord, to winnow away the chaff from my
   heart
and make it like the true wheat
fit to be garnered in thy barn.

—CHINESE PRAYER

**A change of season is a good time to take inven-
tory of life, a good time to ask questions, such
as *Am I growing? Am I becoming more loving,
joyful, peaceful, patient, kind, good, gentle,
faithful, and self-controlled?* Then, take time to
celebrate your progress in areas where there
has been growth. Finally, ask God for the grace
to make further positive changes in your heart.**

October 4 🐚

From the rising of the sun to its setting the name of the Lord is to be praised.
PSALM 113:3

CREATOR GOD, DID YOU intend to make this special kind of sunlight, this special kind of air, and this special kind of mood when you determined that there would be an autumn in your year of seasons? The sunlight is unique; brilliant, but distant. It still reaches us, but it bids us farewell and does so in such a magnificent way. I would not wish for one thing to be different this season, except that it might last just a bit longer. But then that is its charm, isn't it? To come for just a brief time and then to leave us with the wonder of its memory. I love the way you've planned the world, Lord. I love this autumn sunshine.

There is a harmony
In autumn, and a lustre in its sky,
Which through the summer is not heard or seen,
As if it could not be, as if it had not been!
—PERCY BYSSHE SHELLEY, "HYMN TO INTELLECTUAL BEAUTY"

October 5

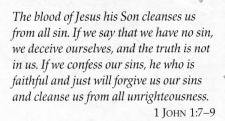

*The blood of Jesus his Son cleanses us
from all sin. If we say that we have no sin,
we deceive ourselves, and the truth is not
in us. If we confess our sins, he who is
faithful and just will forgive us our sins
and cleanse us from all unrighteousness.*

1 JOHN 1:7–9

*D*EAR LORD, early autumn is a time of wondrous beauty, especially the leaves, which turn to radiant fire and glimmering gold. Please remind me that just as the leaves change their color, so also you are changing my heart because of what Jesus did for me on the cross.

**Autumn is a season of reflection, of response to
God, and of remembering his grace and goodness.
Let him soothe your spirit, cleanse your heart, and
transform your thoughts with his love.**

*You have made the moon to mark the
seasons; the sun knows its time for setting.*
PSALM 104:19

WHILE THE LEAVES are falling, vistas open
up once again, dear Lord. I see more of the
beyond, and in the heavens on a clear night,
I can see the stars stretch out before me. You
remind me with this light that you are light.
You illuminate truth to me, and you light my
way. Your presence shines in my heart, bringing me comfort in the dark times and places
of my life. Thank you for the sun, the moon,
and the stars—the lights in the
heavens that I see more clearly
this season—for they reflect the
light of your love. Amen.

October 7

He it is who makes the clouds rise at the end of the earth; ... and brings out the wind from his storehouses.

PSALM 135:7

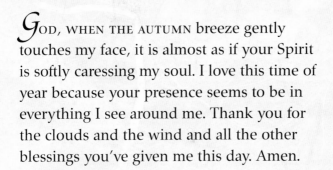

GOD, WHEN THE AUTUMN breeze gently touches my face, it is almost as if your Spirit is softly caressing my soul. I love this time of year because your presence seems to be in everything I see around me. Thank you for the clouds and the wind and all the other blessings you've given me this day. Amen.

Let your hair down; feel the autumn wind blow through it. Carry a kite to the park, and let the winds lift it to the sky. Listen to the song of a wind chime or the gusts whistling through the tree branches. Let the autumn wind bless you today.

October 8

Be exalted, O God, above the heavens,
and let your glory be over all the earth.
PSALM 108:5

HEAVENLY FATHER, WHEN I WALK outside in the October weather, I can't help but praise you. Even when it's rainy, there's something exceptionally beautiful about this time of year. All of my adjectives fail when I want to describe early autumn. I can't quite articulate the effect it has on my heart and mind, but I do know that you understand. For you made the season, and you made me. I just wanted to tell you today that I clearly see your glory during this time of year, and I long to give you an adequate accolade. However, since words fail me, please look into my heart and know how deeply and truly grateful I am.

There is no season when such pleasant and sunny spots may be lighted on, and produce so pleasant an effect on the feelings, as now in October.
—NATHANIEL HAWTHORNE, *AMERICAN NOTE-BOOKS*

 *October 9*

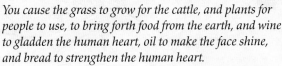

*You cause the grass to grow for the cattle, and plants for
people to use, to bring forth food from the earth, and wine
to gladden the human heart, oil to make the face shine,
and bread to strengthen the human heart.*

Psalm 104:14–15

O Lord, I want to praise you and thank you for providing me with all I need to enjoy this world you created.
How wonderful are these many blessings! God, show me
how to share this joy with everyone I meet today. I don't
want to overwhelm them with the happiness I feel, but I
pray I can be a positive influence on them. Amen.

**Our truest gratitude to God is expressed when we
freely share with others what he has freely given us.**

*Then Jesus told them a parable about their
need to pray always and not to lose heart.*

LUKE 18:1

*H*EAVENLY FATHER, I AM BEGINNING to
know how much I miss when I fail to talk
to thee in prayer, and through prayer to
receive into my life the strength and the
guidance which only thou canst give.
Forgive me for the pride and the presump-
tion that make me continue to struggle to
manage my own affairs to the exhaustion
of my body, the weariness of my mind,
the trail of my faith.

—PETER MARSHALL

**When we neglect to pray, we
are the losers, not God.**

October 11

All scripture is inspired by God and is useful for teaching ... so that everyone who belongs to God may be proficient, equipped for every good work.

2 TIMOTHY 3:16–17

$\mathcal{N}$O MATTER HOW OFTEN we turn to your Word, Lord, we are humbled by the fresh wisdom we glean from it for our lives. Your promise is that your Word will be a lamp to guide our feet every single time. For that we give you praise and thanks.

By the reading of the Scripture, I am so renewed that all nature seems renewed around and with me. The sky seems a purer, a cooler blue, the trees a deeper green, light is sharper on the outlines of the forest and the hills, and the whole world is charged with the glory of God.

—THOMAS MERTON, *THE SIGN OF JONAS*

October 12

You shall love your neighbor as yourself.
MATTHEW 22:39

*L*ORD, I often want to conform the people closest to me to my own image of who they should be. Please forgive me. Help me allow them to be themselves. Help me to love them, to be patient, kind, not envious, not boastful, not arrogant, not rude. Help me not to be irritable or resentful toward them, not to rejoice when they stumble, but to cheer them toward truth. Help me, for their sakes, to bear all things, believe all things, hope all things, and endure all things. Even if they never change to my liking, help me to love them and let them be who they are.

Love consists in this, that two solitudes protect and touch and greet each other. Once the realisation is accepted that even between the closest human beings infinite distances continue to exist, a wonderful living side by side can grow up, if they succeed in loving the distance between them which makes it possible for each to see the other whole against the sky.
—RAINER MARIA RILKE

October 13

One who forgives an affront fosters friendship, but one who dwells on disputes will alienate a friend.

PROVERBS 17:9

*G*OD, AS MUCH AS I DON'T want to, I can't help but listen to your love, which calls me to always seek to make my enemies my friends. How I have grown to truly dislike the call of this love! I would rather love a stranger than an enemy. This is not easy to even want to do! But, still I know that this is what you want me to do in order to make your love real in my life. And so, Lord, flood me with your love because this call is a hard one for me. Amen.

Forging bonds of friendship with those we dislike makes a vast difference in how each day of our lives goes.

*Jesus said, "In everything do to others as you would have
them do to you; for this is the law and the prophets."*
                                    MATTHEW 7:12

$\mathcal{N}$EW VISION, O GOD, is
what this world sorely needs.
Tempers flare and violence
erupts over the most trivial
matters. Remind us that each
one of us is made in your
image and that your people
must extend the hand of
peace if we are to truly be
your ambassadors of peace.

**If we could read the secret history of our enemies,
we should find in each person's life sorrow and
suffering enough to disarm all hostility.**
                        —HENRY WADSWORTH LONGFELLOW

October 15

As God's chosen ones, holy and beloved,
clothe yourselves with compassion, kindness,
humility, meekness, and patience.

COLOSSIANS 3:12

IT MUST BE THE HUMAN condition, Lord, to want to stand out and be the center of attention, but I want to be a member of your orchestra, to play melodies and symphonies that don't focus on my singular abilities but that instead focus on the music you've written. I am choosing to step into the orchestra pit and take my chair. I trust in the Master Conductor to use my talents and blend my sound. And when the time comes for me to play, I trust that it will be used to enhance your music.

When the orchestra begins its concert, should the violin strike up its own version? or the drum? or the oboe? or the trombone? What discord there would be if the Conductor did not lead all the instrumentalists to play together. And that is what must occur in the church: God must lead us as we serve together in harmony.

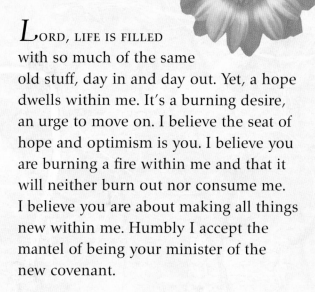
*Our competence is from God, who has made us
competent to be ministers of a new covenant.*
2 CORINTHIANS 3:5–6

LORD, LIFE IS FILLED
with so much of the same
old stuff, day in and day out. Yet, a hope
dwells within me. It's a burning desire,
an urge to move on. I believe the seat of
hope and optimism is you. I believe you
are burning a fire within me and that it
will neither burn out nor consume me.
I believe you are about making all things
new within me. Humbly I accept the
mantel of being your minister of the
new covenant.

**Optimism, which is hope in action, is truly a powerful tool for
building the future, for it releases the awesome possibilities God
has in mind for making things new within and without.**

October 17

A false balance is an abomination to the Lord, but an accurate weight is his delight.

GOD, I SAW A CHILD wobbling on one of those adult-size bicycles, and it occurred to me: Maybe, I'm like that child when I unsuccessfully try to balance the demands of this world with the demands of your Spirit. God, help me balance the two. I am utterly incapable of keeping my balance on my own. I need your hand on me to guide me. Please steer me in the direction you want me to go.

God restores balance when we're about to fall, for he will always keep us upright in all that we do as long as we remain obedient to his will and Word.

God said, *"Ask what I should give you."*
1 Kings 3:5

Goᴅ, ʜᴏᴡ ᴅᴏ I ᴋɴᴏᴡ what I really
need? I thought I could show up at your
doorstep and then you would provide me
with all my needs. This seems so reminis-
cent of my childhood when I was told to
go do what I could do for myself. Am I
fighting growing up in my faith? Am I
reluctant to be a mature person of faith?
Well, of course! Help me, God, as I
grow into a spiritual adult. Help me
seek and find the strengths that are mine and
dedicate those gifts to your service as they
were intended since the beginning of time.
I will be renewed in serving you. Amen.

**Renewal will not visit us; we
must go find it.**

October 19

Let love be genuine; hate what is evil, hold fast to what is good.

ROMANS 12:9

GOOD CAN BE SO BORING, God. And God, evil hides so easily in the thrill of the moment and in the pause that seems to refresh. Help me look deep into myself that I might find the strength to hold on for the long race, the long haul that is demanded of the faithful life, which ends with the phrase: "Well done, good and faithful servant." God, I need help discovering the joy of discipline that will strengthen me to hold fast to what is good and to always shun evil.

October 20

GOD HELP MY THOUGHTS! They stray from me, setting off on the wildest journeys....

They come to me for a fleeting moment, and then away they flee. No chains, no locks can hold them back; no threats of punishment can restrain them....

They slip from my grasp like tails of eels; they swoop hither and thither like swallows in flight.

Dear, chaste Christ, who can see into every heart and read every mind, take hold of my thoughts. Bring my thoughts back to me, and clasp me to yourself.

—CELTIC PRAYER, "A SCHOLAR'S WISH"

**Thoughts are the main ingredient
in the recipe for behavior.**

October 21

Hatred stirs up strife, but love covers all offenses.
PROVERBS 10:12

*M*Y BIGGEST FEAR, God, is that in loving people who vigorously oppose you, I will have failed to stand against the injustices they have perpetrated against the innocent and defenseless ones they have harmed. How do I stand firmly and clearly for justice and yet still love your enemies? Does my love cloak their iniquities? I know in my soul that I must love those people, but still, God, I wonder and fear that love is much too easy. Strengthen me to be able to love them and give me wisdom to know how to extend your love without compromising your justice.

**The fire you kindle for your enemy
often burns you more than him.**
—CHINESE PROVERB

October 22

Jesus said, "Simon, Simon, listen! Satan has demanded to sift all of you like wheat, but I have prayed for you that your own faith may not fail; and you, when once you have turned back, strengthen your brothers."

LUKE 22:31

DEAR GOD, THANK YOU with all my heart for the wonderful gifts of friendship You have given me over a lifetime. Please alert me by Your Spirit to those in special need, both in sustained intercession and in practical ways. Increase my understanding of my privileges and responsibilities in prayer on their behalf. Thank You that You will. In Jesus' name, Amen.

—JOY DAWSON, *INTERCESSION*

Make a list of friends for whom you will pray today. Then let them know that you have prayed for them. Perhaps in talking with them, you will learn how God has answered your prayers for them.

October 23

Consider your own call, brothers and sisters: not many of you were wise by human standards, not many were powerful, not many were of noble birth. But God chose... things that are not [powerful or noble], to reduce to nothing the things that are, so that no one might boast in the presence of God.

1 Corinthians 1:26–29

LORD, HELP ME DELIGHT in the fact that you have chosen me to be your child. Help me realize that you do not despise me for my weakness. In fact, you have turned my stumbling into a showcase for your great love and transforming power. Thank you for embracing me, failings and all, and for empowering me by your own greatness to be more than I could have ever dreamed of being on my own.

We don't have to worry about how wise or clever we are—God chose the foolish. We don't have to worry about how powerful we are—God chose the weak. We don't have to worry about how popular we are, or even whether we'll amount to anything much—God chose the despised and the ones who were nothing. None of those human measurements counts when it comes to performing great acts in life—great acts as defined by God, acts of humility, obedience, and love.

—Jimmy Carter

Rejoice in hope, be patient in suffering, persevere in prayer.
ROMANS 12:12

*W*HAT COMFORT AND SUPPORT in knowing
that you, like a doting mother, are always
ready to hear about our day—our mundane,
ordinary moments as well as the momentous
and life-changing ones! Lord, we promise to
maintain this habit of talking to you about
whatever is on our minds and in our hearts.

**Nothing about God's children
is too trivial or ordinary, too
overwhelming or dreadful to
be withheld from God. His ear
is as close as a bent knee and
a bowed head.**

October 25

We have gifts that differ according to the grace given to us: prophecy, in proportion to faith; ministry, in ministering; the teacher, in teaching; the exhorter, in exhortation; the giver, in generosity; the leader, in diligence; the compassionate, in cheerfulness.

ROMANS 12:6–8

THE AWARENESS of finding and doing your work with the gifts you've given me blesses me on and off my job. Go with me, O God, into every avenue of my life and show me how to use my unique talents.

A maple leaf is a maple leaf and not a snowflake, and we are human creatures, each one sharing in our humanness, but each one also uniquely different.

—MADELEINE L'ENGLE, *GLIMPSES OF GRACE*

October 26

Jesus said, "Go into all the world and proclaim the good news to the whole creation."

MARK 16:15

*L*ORD, GIVE ME FREEDOM to rejoice in Your gifts of life and love. Lord, give me faith, faith to be happy and to praise You with all my strength.

—JAMES L. CHRISTENSEN, *NEW WAYS TO WORSHIP*

With open, thankful hands, I accept the gifts of freedom and joy as building blocks to my faith in God. Then I will introduce strangers to the God of love, for being his ambassador is an awesome task.

October 27

Little children, let us love, not in word or speech, but in truth and action.

1 JOHN 3:18

*D*EAR HEAVENLY FATHER, I truly want to do good toward others. I don't want to just talk about being good, but I desire to be more compassionate. God, I need for you to teach me to be far more sensitive to the needs and sorrows of the people you have placed in my life and to be kind and encouraging toward them. I need for you to teach me how to truly love. I pray for this with all my heart. Amen.

I have never heard anything about the resolutions of the Apostles, but a great deal about their Acts.

—HORACE MANN

October 28

As far as the east is from the west, so far
he removes our transgressions from us.
PSALM 103:12

SCARCELY A DAY or even an hour goes by, God, that we don't have to confess, "I blew it." Guide us to make amends and restitution, knowing that your forgiveness will give us the courage to do so.

October 29

*So I tell you, whatever you ask for in prayer, believe
that you have received it, and it will be yours.*

MARK 11:24

*H*EAVENLY FATHER, WE PRAY
and hear you answer in the
voice of new thoughts, in
changed perceptions, and in
the helping hand of a friend.
From our knees, we lift our
faces to the sun and feel
autumn's blazing warmth,
and we know that you hear
our every word.

**Every man prays in his own language and there is
no language that God does not understand.**

—DUKE ELLINGTON

October 30

Everyone then who hears these words of mine and acts on them will be like a wise man who built his house on rock. The rain fell, the floods came, and the winds blew and beat on that house, but it did not fall, because it had been founded on rock.

MATTHEW 7:24–25

*D*EAR GOD, FROM WHOM every family receives its true name, I pray for all the members of my family: for those who are growing up, that they may increase in wisdom and love; for those facing changes, that they may meet them with hope; for those who are weak, that they may find strength; for those with heavy burdens, that they may carry them lightly; for those who are old and frail, that they may grow in faith.

—AUTHOR UNKNOWN

More than a house, a love-built home is where the heart dwells when warmed by the steadfast presence of God.

October 31

Jesus looked at them and said, "For mortals it is impossible, but for God all things are possible."
MATTHEW 19:26

*W*HEN WE GROW DISCOURAGED, God, raise our eyes toward spiderwebs spun in a corner and remind us that no hope is too small. At first glance, the webs look like fragile, insignificant strands, but, in fact, they have amazing strength. And consider what those webs do for the spider. They bring it sustenance. Help us twist our own tiny strands of hope into sturdy ropes of commitment when we take the next step toward the tasks you are calling us to. Amen.

My prayer life:

November 1

So then you are no longer strangers and aliens, but you are citizens with the saints and also members of the household of God, built upon the foundation of the apostles and prophets, with Christ Jesus himself as the cornerstone.

EPHESIANS 2:19–20

DEAR LORD, THANK YOU for those men and women whose faith and deeds have built your church. Though some of them have suffered greatly, and have even given their lives as martyrs, they are not forgotten. Even more, I praise your Son who is the head of the church and for what he has done. May I follow in their footsteps, using the skills and talents you have given me to advance your church. Amen.

Seek a quiet corner to give thanks for the saints whose day this celebrates. Remember those pillars of the faith upon whose shoulders we stand. It's too easy to lose track of what we should really celebrate in the commercial darkness of the previous night.

November 2

The Lord will fulfill his purpose for me; your steadfast love, O Lord, endures forever. Do not forsake the work of your hands.

PSALM 138:8

I KNOW AT TIMES, God, that I shrink back when your hands come upon me, but I really do want you to make me into the person you want me to be. Please be patient with me. My utmost desire is to truly please you.

When we turn to the Lord, he will mold us into the people he wants us to be.

November 3

*One generation shall laud your works to another,
and shall declare your mighty acts.*

PSALM 145:4

*H*EAVENLY FATHER, I AM so grateful for the generation of believers before and after me. Those before me have taught me so much about you, and those after me have listened to the spiritual insights you have given me. To be a part of this tradition of passing your grace from one generation to the next is a privilege I truly treasure. Amen.

**The Lord guides each generation into an abundant future.
Meanwhile, he keeps them on the cutting edge of his grace.**

November 4

I am the good shepherd. The good shepherd lays down his life for the sheep.

JOHN 10:11

TONIGHT, GOD, I'll sleep like a contented sheep relaxing in your pasture. I'll lie down and rise up in your care, and I'll be restored, renewed, and rested with the promise that you'll be with me again tomorrow.

The Lord guards our souls and watches over our spiritual health. Indeed, he stands between us and all our enemies.

November 5

Jesus said to him, ... "All things can be done for the one who believes." Immediately the father of the child cried out, "I believe; help my unbelief!"

MARK 9:23–24

*H*OW NEEDLESSLY we get down on ourselves when we think you're angry at us! Help us accept doubts that come, heavenly Father, for they can be magnifying glasses that clarify thoughts, beliefs, and dreams. But also help us get through them so we can be at peace with you.

November 6

For where two or three are gathered in my name, I am there among them.

MATTHEW 18:20

O THOU … I crave Thy heavenly blessing also for all the members of this household, all my neighbours, and all my fellow citizens. Let Christ rule in every heart and His law be honoured in every home. Let every knee be bent before Him and every tongue confess that He is Lord. Amen.

—JOHN BAILLIE, *A DIARY OF PRIVATE PRAYER*

God is our planner and builder. May there be laughter, love, and strength in our homes. May it be a sanctuary. May God bless those we live with and all who visit us. And may we, like God, always offer shelter and welcome.

November 7

Then someone came to [Jesus] and said, "Teacher, what good deed must I do to have eternal life?"... Jesus said to him, "... sell your possessions, and give the money to the poor, ... then come, follow me." When the young man heard this word, he went away grieving, for he had many possessions.

MATTHEW 19:16, 21–22

*D*EAR LORD, TEACH ME to be generous; teach me to serve you as you deserve; to give and not to count the cost... to toil and not to seek for rest, to labor and not to seek reward, except that of knowing that I do your will.

—SAINT IGNATIUS OF LOYOLA

November 8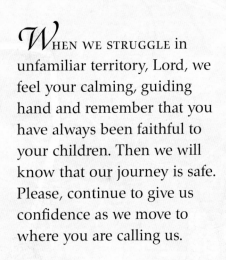

I am the Lord, I have called you in righteousness, I have taken you by the hand and kept you; I have given you as a covenant to the people, a light to the nations.

ISAIAH 42:1

WHEN WE STRUGGLE in unfamiliar territory, Lord, we feel your calming, guiding hand and remember that you have always been faithful to your children. Then we will know that our journey is safe. Please, continue to give us confidence as we move to where you are calling us.

Let us not curse our luck when we get lost, but let us take God's hand, for surely he will reveal the best route for us as we travel in this world.

November 9

Your word is a lamp to my feet and a light to my path.

PSALM 119:105

How COMFORTING AND inspiring to know, Lord, that we aren't the first to travel roads pitted with questions, doubts, and temptations! Point us to your marvelous Word, where we can join hands with our ancestors of faith and link the foundation of the past with the potential of the future.

The Bible is alive, it speaks to me; it has feet, it runs after me; it has hands, it lays hold on me.

—MARTIN LUTHER

If two lie together, they keep warm; but how can one keep
warm alone? And though one might prevail against another,
two will withstand one. A threefold cord is not quickly broken.

ECCLESIASTES 4:11–12

$\mathcal{G}$OD, ENCOURAGEMENT through friends and family lifts my heart just as sunshine turns roses skyward. Despite the chill of autumn, may their love inspire me to stretch my soul toward the warmth and nurture of your radiant affection for me.

The thread of our life would be dark, heaven knows, if it were not with friendship and love intertwined.

—SIR THOMAS MORE, *FRIENDSHIP IS A SPECIAL GIFT*

November 11

[The righteous] are like trees planted by streams of water, which yield their fruit in its season, and their leaves do not wither. In all that they do, they prosper. The wicked are not so, but are like chaff that the wind drives away.

PSALM 1:3–4

TEACH ME, O GOD, so to use all the circumstances of my life to-day that they may bring forth in me the fruits of holiness rather than the fruits of sin. Let me use disappointment as material for patience: Let me use success as material for thankfulness: Let me use suspense as material for perseverance: Let me use danger as material for courage: Let me use reproach as material for long-suffering: Let me use praise as material for humility: Let me use pleasures as material for temperance: Let me use pains as material for endurance.

—JOHN BAILLIE, *A DIARY OF PRIVATE PRAYER*

It is only by living completely in this world that one learns to have faith…By this worldliness I mean living unreservedly in life's duties, problems, successes and failures, experiences and perplexities. In so doing we throw ourselves completely into the arms of God, taking seriously, not our own suffering, but those of God in the world.

—JAMES L. CHRISTENSEN, *CREATIVE WAYS TO WORSHIP*

November 12

His master said to him, "Well done, good and trustworthy
slave; you have been trustworthy in a few things, I will put you
in charge of many things; enter into the joy of your master."

MATTHEW 25:23

BLESS US, O LORD, as we toss ourselves,
unique talents and all, into the stream of
life, as if called to make ripples wherever
we are. Use us to spread love, which is a
gift that keeps making ever-widening
circles eventually reaching even those
stranded on the edge of the shore.

November 13

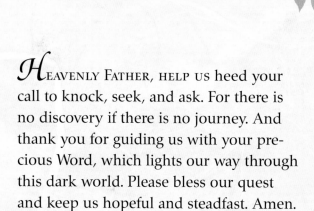

For whatever was written in former days was written for our instruction, so that by steadfastness and by the encouragement of the scriptures we might have hope.

ROMANS 15:4

*H*EAVENLY FATHER, HELP US heed your call to knock, seek, and ask. For there is no discovery if there is no journey. And thank you for guiding us with your precious Word, which lights our way through this dark world. Please bless our quest and keep us hopeful and steadfast. Amen.

You were like me, Jesus....It comforts me knowing that I am not alone in this human valley, for I saw your footprints in it.
—JAMES L. CHRISTENSEN, *CREATIVE WAYS TO WORSHIP*

Pray without ceasing.
1 THESSALONIANS 5:17

A STURDY BRIDGE, prayer connects us to you, God, who is always first to celebrate our joys and first to weep at our troubles. It is in this sharing that love brings about its most miraculous ways and we are lifted above the trials and tribulations of life. Thank you, Lord.

"Prayer was never meant to be magic," Mother said. "Then why bother with it?" Suzy scowled. "Because it's an act of love," Mother said.
—MADELEINE L'ENGLE, *GLIMPSES OF GRACE*

November 15

Your righteousness is like the mighty
mountains, your judgments are like
the great deep; you save humans and
animals alike, O Lord.

PSALM 36:6

OUR MOST HOLY CREATOR, we are grateful that you placed us in the company of mammals, birds, and fish. They are all your creatures—both great and small. Sharing a home—either our own four walls or the whole world—with them blesses us. Make us worthy of their trust.

The underfoot affection for and from beloved pets keeps me moving when I would rather sit and reminds me I'm loved when I feel otherwise.

November 16

*Do not rejoice when your enemies
fall, and do not let your heart be glad
when they stumble.*

PROVERBS 24:17

*G*OD, PLEASE GIVE US wisdom, and yes,
courage to feel sympathy, not glee, when
someone we dislike encounters trouble.
Help us refrain from celebrating the misfortune of others, even when we feel that
it is deserved. Instead, give us compassionate hearts so that we might faithfully
follow the footsteps of your Son.

**Small deeds of goodness in the aftermath of
trouble, like fireflies flickering against a dark sky,
can blanket the world with sparkling lights.**

November 17

No testing has overtaken you that is not common to everyone. God is faithful, and he will not let you be tested beyond your strength, but with the testing he will also provide the way out so that you may be able to endure it.

1 CORINTHIANS 10:13

LORD, WHEN THE GOOD that you desire for us isn't possible because we are beset with staggering problems, it is enough to know that you are still there for us with comfort, support, and inspiration. We also know that you want us to conquer those problems and that you will provide the strength we need to ultimately be victorious.

November 18 🐚

I will both lie down and sleep in peace; for you alone, O Lord, make me lie down in safety.

PSALM 4:8

*G*IVE ME SOUND AND refreshing sleep: Give me safety from all perils: Give me in my sleep freedom from rest-less dreams: Give me control of my thoughts, if I should lie awake: Give me wisdom to remember that the night was made for sleeping, and not for the harbouring of anxious or fretful or shameful thoughts. Give me grace, if as I lie abed I think at all, to think upon Thee.

—JOHN BAILLIE, *A DIARY OF PRIVATE PRAYER*

The Lord of quiet pastures and still waters can help us relinquish our relentless hold on details at home and work; he provides a delightful world for our times of rest.

November 19

For now we see in a mirror, dimly, but then we will see face to face. Now I know only in part; then I will know fully, even as I have been fully known.

1 CORINTHIANS 13:12

HELP US LIVE WITH MYSTERY, O God, for within each question is the possibility of growth, wisdom, and a deeper faith. For with you, we find courage to ask the questions, trusting that sometime, maybe without even noticing it, we will discover the answers.

November 20

No one who conceals transgressions will prosper, but one who confesses and forsakes them will obtain mercy.

PROVERBS 28:13

O GOD, TEACH US TO know that failure is as much a part of life as success—and whether it shall be evil or good depends upon the way we meet it—if we face it listlessly and faint-heartedly, angrily or vengefully, then indeed is it evil…but if we let our failures stand as guideposts and as warnings—as beacons and as guardians—then is honest failure far better than stolen success, and but a part of that great training which God gives us to make us men and women. The race is not to the swift—nor the battle to the strong, O God. Amen.

—W.E.B. DU BOIS, *HEAL YOUR SOUL, HEAL THE WORLD*

When failures come, learn from them, for if you do, you won't be a failure.

🐚 *November 21*

So then, whenever we have an opportunity, let us work for the good of all, and especially for those of the family of faith.

GALATIANS 6:10

$\mathcal{H}$OW OFTEN WE CRITICIZE and turn away from people with seemingly unusual behavior, O God, not knowing they, like a fish on a line, are snagged on one of life's hooks. Help us look beneath the surface instead of condemning and rejecting. May we then unhook their snagged hand and draw them closer to you.

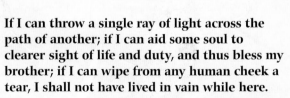

If I can throw a single ray of light across the path of another; if I can aid some soul to clearer sight of life and duty, and thus bless my brother; if I can wipe from any human cheek a tear, I shall not have lived in vain while here.

—ANONYMOUS

November 22

You saw how the Lord your God carried you,
just as one carries a child, all the way that you
traveled until you reached this place.

DEUTERONOMY 1:31

THANK YOU, O LORD, for being my companion throughout the day. Though many things are pulling me in many directions, I know you will keep me on course to do what is truly important. Thank you as well for listening to me and counseling me when I need to verbally unwind or when I need advice. This I pray. Amen.

Spanning the often murky waters of daily life, faith forms a sturdy bridge so that we can cross holding tightly to the rope of courage in one hand and God in the other.

November 23

If you will only heed his every commandment…he will give the rain for your land in its season…and you will gather in your grain, your wine, and your oil; and he will give grass in your fields for your livestock, and you will eat your fill.

DEUTERONOMY 11:13–15

LORD, WE THANK YOU for the daily bread you provide us in so many ways, some we are not even aware of. Help us not only to always be grateful for your blessings but also to always be obedient to your Word, which is a great blessing in itself. We promise to strive to be always right with you so we can fully enjoy the abundant life you have given us.

November 24

Even the darkness is not dark to you; the night is as bright as the day, for darkness is as light to you.

PSALM 139:12

I T'S HARD, O LORD, to change. To give up that which is desirable to us is like giving up sun-warmed air for frost-chilled air. Nevertheless, thank you for surrounding us—even as close as our own back-yards—with the reassuring message that you have a purpose for everything, even approaching winters.

Evidence of frost is on the piling leaves, twigs, and debris scattered throughout the garden. Yet, we know that the work done in fall will be easily seen come spring.

November 25

God blessed them, and God said to them, "Be fruitful and multiply, and fill the earth and subdue it; and have dominion over the fish of the sea and over the birds of the air and over every living thing that moves upon the earth."

GENESIS 1:28

HEAVENLY CREATOR, BRING TO US an awareness of how we can better live in harmony with your creation. This awareness is the first step in redeeming the harm done to the world, which you gave us to tend. Spring us into action so that we can become your instruments to heal the damage we see around us. Teach us to truly love what you have made. It all starts with picking up that first scrap of litter in my own backyard.

The main reason for healing is love.
—PARACELSUS

November 26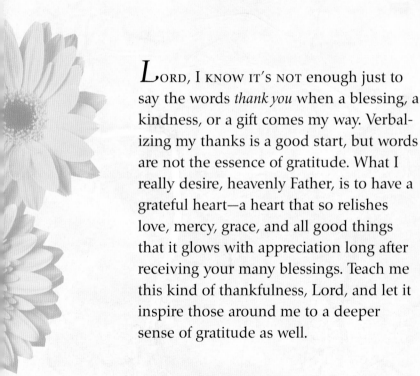

Offer to God a sacrifice of thanksgiving.
PSALM 50:14

LORD, I KNOW IT'S NOT enough just to
say the words *thank you* when a blessing, a
kindness, or a gift comes my way. Verbal-
izing my thanks is a good start, but words
are not the essence of gratitude. What I
really desire, heavenly Father, is to have a
grateful heart—a heart that so relishes
love, mercy, grace, and all good things
that it glows with appreciation long after
receiving your many blessings. Teach me
this kind of thankfulness, Lord, and let it
inspire those around me to a deeper
sense of gratitude as well.

**Thankful spirits will arise out of a pattern
of thankfulness set in the home.**

—ANN HIBBARD

November 27

Make a joyful noise to the Lord, all the earth. Worship the Lord with gladness; come into his presence with singing.

Know that the Lord is God. It is he that made us, and we are his; we are his people, and the sheep of his pasture.

Enter his gates with thanksgiving, and his courts with praise. Give thanks to him, bless his name. For the Lord is good; his steadfast love endures forever, and his faithfulness to all generations.

PSALM 100

I PRAISE YOU, LORD, with all my heart.

I see and smell and hear and feel the creativity of God this fall season. As my soul revels in the blessing of the wonders of his earth, may I seek creative ways to express my praise.

November 28

I will call to mind the deeds of the Lord; I will remember your wonders of old.

THIS IS AN appropriate time, Lord, for me to take personal inventory of all your blessings. I think first of relationships with which you've filled my life. These are most meaningful, and I'm grateful for the time you've granted with the ones I love. Then there is my health, my home, my income, and my faith. Today I'll spend some time reflecting on such things, and as I do, may I gain an even deeper appreciation for your presence in my life. For you are truly my Father, the one who cares for me in every way.

Gratitude is the memory of the heart.
—J. B. MASSIEU, LETTER TO THE ABBE SICARD

November 29

Rejoice always, ... give thanks in all circumstances; for this is the will of God in Christ Jesus for you.

1 THESSALONIANS 5:16, 18

WHETHER OR NOT THINGS in my life right now are ideal, Lord, there's so much to thank you for. Each meal I eat, each day I see, and each breath I take comes from your gracious hand. And there are so many more blessings besides these, but help me not forget that even these basic gifts are not to be taken for granted.

In fairness, if we ask the "Why me?" question in regard to our burdens, we should also ask it in regard to our blessings. For this is the other side of the coin.... There are many times in life when we do have both the occasion and the opportunity to ask "Why me?" in response to life's bountiful blessings. The Thanksgiving season is but one.

—DALE TURNER

November 30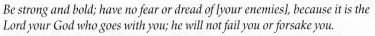

Be strong and bold; have no fear or dread of [your enemies], because it is the Lord your God who goes with you; he will not fail you or forsake you.

DEUTERONOMY 31:6

LORD, I AM NOT normally a brave person. So many things frighten me. I am especially afraid of being alone with my problems. Give me the courage to meet the challenges I encounter each day, and help me to know that you are with me, and therefore, I have nothing to fear.

My prayer life:

_____

_____

_____

_____

_____

_____

_____

_____

_____

_____

_____

_____

December 1

Like newborn infants, long for the pure, spiritual milk, so that by it you may grow into salvation.

1 PETER 2:2

*H*EAVENLY FATHER, we yearn to grow in our faith. As your children, we pray that we can mature spiritually into the men and women you want us to be. Nourish us with your love and your wisdom, and shelter us with your heavenly parental care.

Just as toddlers do, we take a few small steps forward each day and try to relish the moments. By focusing on one day at a time, eventually we can look *back* and we are amazed at how far we've come on this bumpy road.

—JAN MARKELL, *WAITING FOR A MIRACLE*

December 2

In the same way, faith by itself, if it is not accompanied by action, is dead.

JAMES 2:17, NIV

$\mathcal{W}$E PUT OFF, cop out, and stall, O God, instead of just answering your summons to put action to our words and hands to our thoughts. Forgive us for being so lazy. Increase our faith so we can step out boldly, knowing that you are always with us with your strength, your wisdom, and your love. Amen.

Often we…make excuses for our inaction. It's not the right time. I can't make a difference. We must ask God's forgiveness and help to keep being useful in small ways.

—MARIAN WRIGHT EDELMAN

December 3

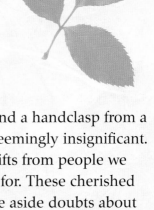

Therefore encourage one another and build up each other, as indeed you are doing.

1 THESSALONIANS 5:11

GOD, A CALL, a note, and a handclasp from a friend are simple and seemingly insignificant. Yet, you inspire these gifts from people we have a special affection for. These cherished acts of friendship nudge aside doubts about who we are when we feel low and encourage our hearts in a way that lifts our spirits. Thank you for the friends you have given us.

After the friendship of God, a friend's affection is the greatest treasure here below.

—ANONYMOUS

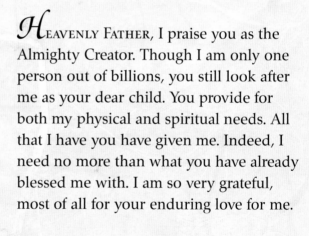

December 4

Great are the works of the Lord, studied by all who delight in them.... the Lord is gracious and merciful. He provides food for those who fear him.

PSALM 111:2, 4–5

*H*EAVENLY FATHER, I praise you as the Almighty Creator. Though I am only one person out of billions, you still look after me as your dear child. You provide for both my physical and spiritual needs. All that I have you have given me. Indeed, I need no more than what you have already blessed me with. I am so very grateful, most of all for your enduring love for me.

When we look carefully, we can trace all good gifts back to God. He leaves his divine fingerprints as evidence.

December 5 🐚

For David says..., "I saw the Lord always before me, for he is at my right hand so that I will not be shaken...my flesh will live in hope."

ACTS 2:25–26

*P*OISED AT THE threshold of each new day, we wonder what it will bring and who we will become. O God, we eagerly move forward into what you have in store for us, filled not with fear but with a vibrant hope that fuels growth and gratitude. Amen.

December 6

*See, I have set before you today life and
prosperity, death and adversity....
blessings and curses. Choose life so that
you and your descendants may live.*

DEUTERONOMY 30:15, 19

LORD, I DO HAVE this life! I do
want to live it to the full. Don't let
me miss anything good. Keep my
thoughts from wandering. Cause
me to heed how I hear Your Word.
Give me understanding that I may
receive the message You send.
Open my mind and heart that I
may communicate and respond.

—JAMES L. CHRISTENSEN, *NEW WAYS TO WORSHIP*

**The life we live today is tomorrow's home
movie. The choices we make will be the images
flickering across memory's screen, both tasks
completed and relationships nurtured.**

December 7 🐚

He will cover you with his pinions, and under his wings you will find refuge.

PSALM 91:4

*D*ESPITE THE SUDDEN thunderstorm, Creator God, the cardinal refuses to move, standing like a mighty shelter over her fledglings beneath her outstretched wings. We are grateful that you hover over us and protect us during life's storms because you love us in the same way that a mother loves her children.

How comforting to know that God tends us while we move through life's extremes—in stillness and activity! We cannot wander so far in any direction that God is not already there.

December 8

For everything created by God is good,
and nothing is to be rejected.

1 TIMOTHY 4:4

O LORD, HOW CAN I be more amazed than by seeing you use everything for your good? At times, when I think things are not going right or when others trouble me with their problems, still you are involved, moving my life toward the goal you have set forth before me. Help me, I pray, to be more trusting. Amen.

Faith offers a new way of life, where everything can be used for good. Like a tilting kaleidoscope, our days are arranged with different priorities. It's amazing how little the dusty tabletop matters when close friends come to call.

For I am convinced that neither death, nor life, nor angels, nor rulers, nor things present, nor things to come, nor powers, nor height, nor depth, nor anything else in all creation, will be able to separate us from the love of God in Christ Jesus our Lord.

ROMANS 8:38–39

O GOD, IN THE GRACE and strength that You daily grant, Your servants find reason for celebration. You have truly fulfilled our innermost longings. You have responded to our deepest needs. We raise our voices in praise, O God, because no one can separate us from You.

—LESLIE F. BRANDT

I will tell you, I have heard ... God has two dwellings, one in heaven and the other in the meek and thankful heart.

—IZAK WALTON

December 10

*All the days of the afflicted are evil: but he that
is of a merry heart hath a continual feast.*
PROVERBS 15:15, KJV

GOD, WE CONFESS that our thoughts and
beliefs can be for us either outstretched
wings or prison bars. Save us from the
downward spiral in which we think
defeating thoughts, become depressed,
and then act in hopeless ways, reinforcing
our negative beliefs. Break the cycle, O
Lord! Set us free from ideas that imprison
our minds and shackle our actions.
Restore us to balance so we may soar
through the peaks and the valleys with
outstretched wings. Amen.

We are governed not by armies or police, but by ideas.
—MONA CAIRD, REVOLUTION FROM WITHIN

December 11

O give thanks to the Lord, for he is good, for his steadfast love endures forever. O give thanks to the God of gods, for his steadfast love endures forever. O give thanks to the Lord of lords, for his steadfast love endures forever.

PSALM 136:1–3

GOD, THERE IS SO MUCH pleasure in your creation. Our senses delight in the flavors of our favorite foods, in the sounds of laughter around our tables, in the smells of the fireplace blazing and apple pie warming, in the touch of a baby's hand on our face and a puppy's tongue on our toes, and in the snapshots of living that connect us to loved ones, pictures to replay in our minds like slides on a screen. May our gratitude overflow into the deprived spaces in the world. May we create lyrics for songs of praise with those who are too hungry to sing. Help us be good stewards of your blessings, relishing them all the more as we pass them on to others.

Were there no God, we would be in this glorious world with grateful hearts: and no one to thank.

—CHRISTINA ROSSETTI

December 12

See, I have inscribed you on the palms of my hands.

ISAIAH 49:16

*H*EAVENLY FATHER, I forgot the car keys, and I need to get to my appointments in time. It's hard to remember every detail in my life. Yet, unlike us, who need reminders like dates engraved inside wedding bands to remember anniversaries or strings around fingers to keep up with tasks, you know every little detail of our lives. Thank you for keeping us foremost in your thoughts.

Moving ahead, even from comfort and familiarity, is merely accepting the invitation to become all I can be; God's hand holds the invitation.

December 13

Jesus said, "Abide in me as I abide in you. Just as the branch cannot bear fruit by itself unless it abides in the vine, neither can you unless you abide in me. I am the vine, you are the branches. Those who abide in me and I in them bear much fruit."

JOHN 15:4–5

DEAR GOD, I WANT TO abide in you, but sometimes it's not easy. I feel so stubborn—I want to do things my own way. Yet, I know that when you abide in me, that's when my life is sailing safely on any kind of waters. Teach me to be more willing to abide in you as you abide in me, for I know that this is definitely the best course for me. Amen.

God has made us so that we do best that which he inspires within us.

December 14

Go your way… for the joy of the Lord is your strength.
NEHEMIAH 8:10

*W*HAT JOY IT IS, GOD, to open my mind up to your wisdom, to open the door to a new opportunity, and to open my hands to yours when I need you to pull me to another task! Thank you for opening up your joy to me.

Put action to hope in the same way a puppy eagerly paws a hard, summer-parched ground. Sooner or later, something surprising—a fresh solution, a new direction, a long-buried idea—may be unearthed. Even an old bone has value!

May the Lord give strength to his people!
May the Lord bless his people with peace!
PSALM 29:11

$\mathcal{W}$E GO TO BED at night, heads swirling with
things that need to be done, worries, problems
to solve, all manner of concerns. We lie awake,
spinning schemes to save, to solve, to win, to
get ahead. And sleep is sometimes an elusive
stranger even though your scriptures promise
that you give your loved ones sleep. We confess,
O Lord, that we can't stop thinking that it is all
up to us. We can't lay down our burdens at your
feet because we do not yet trust you. Give us
that peace that soothes and calms but is beyond
our understanding. And let us lie down and rise
up with this peace as our constant companion.

—CHARLES CAMMARATA, *LIGHTING THE FLAME*

December 16

ETERNAL GOD, You are in our midst and are always ready to hear our prayers. You already know our innermost longings and are aware of our needs. Our perpetual need is for Your mercy and love. We reach for Your forgiving love and claim anew Your gracious acceptance.

—LESLIE F. BRANDT

Although God already knows what is in our hearts and on our minds, he desires that we express these feelings and thoughts to him. He wants to listen to our words so he then can assure us of his intimate concern for us by answering our prayers with his grace, acceptance, and blessings.

I will seek the lost, and I will bring back the strayed, and I will bind up the injured, and I will strengthen the weak.
EZEKIEL 34:16

O GOD, DURING THIS SEASON of giving, awake in our hearts the desire to give practical provisions to those in need. You call on us not to contemplate what others and you can give to us. Instead, teach us that our joy increases not because of the presents that are placed in our arms, but rather because of the gifts we hand to others, especially those who can never repay us.

Give what you have. To some it may be better than you dare think.
—HENRY WADSWORTH LONGFELLOW

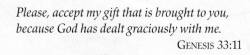# *December 18*

Please, accept my gift that is brought to you,
because God has dealt graciously with me.

GENESIS 33:11

*H*EAVENLY FATHER, we are surrounded
at this time of year with messages that
both urge us to give and compel us to
want. And yet, as the presents pile up
underneath the tree, they cannot reach
the emptiness that echoes in our hearts.
Fill us up, not with things wrapped in foil
and bows, but with conversations, memories shared, memorable moments, kindness, and laughter. Help us to reach out to
re-establish lost connections and to be
open to receiving touches from unexpected places. Amen.

**God asks only that we drop whatever we're so busy about these
days to accept a gesture so small that it may get overlooked. All
it takes is a willingness to let a small hand take ours.**

December 19

The testing of your faith produces endurance.

LORD, THERE ARE TIMES when I find praying difficult and your answers elusive. I struggle to find and connect with you. Instead, I hear only my own words echoing back, and so my confusion increases. Help me, O God, to change my prayers. Instead of asking "Why?" Help me to ask "What? What do I need to do now? What can I learn from this?" Then empower me with your Spirit to respond to your answers as you want me to.

December 20

For those who want to save their life will lose it, and those who lose their life for my sake, and for the sake of the gospel, will save it.

MARK 8:35

DEAR LORD, help us relax during one of the longest, darkest nights of the year, knowing that in order for trees to blossom and bear fruit and the maple tree to yield its sugar, a resting stillness is necessary. Thank you for also giving us fertile fields, flowering gardens, and warm rain, even as we mourn their absence. Let this be a time of reflection. Help us celebrate the paradox that it is only by giving ourselves away that we find ourselves brimming over with the fruits of your Spirit.

December 21

You show me the path of life. In your presence there is fullness of joy; in your right hand are pleasures forevermore.

PSALM 16:11

O GOD, WHY DO WE STRAY from your path? Every time we do, we lose our balance and fall. We get so busy that we become lopsided. Guide us so we can make free time in our tight schedules and then become gifts of grace to our families, friends, and even ourselves. Help us live as fully as you intended.

Seek not abroad, turn back into thy self for in the inner man dwells the truth.

—SAINT AUGUSTINE, *CITY OF GOD*

December 22

Be strong, and let your heart take courage, all you who wait for the Lord.

PSALM 31:24

*G*OD, I KNOW you're with me as I press on through the bleak times and through the difficult issues I face—especially the ones that never seem to find a happy ending. It is precisely because you are with me that I can press on. Thank you for the winters of the soul, for they draw me close to you and cause me to remember your promises and that your Word brings me hope. I know that joy will return to my heart one day, but until then, I'll keep warm in your reassuring presence.

If winter comes, can spring be far behind?
—PERCY SHELLEY, "ODE TO THE WEST WIND"

December 23

But now the Lord my God has given me rest on every side; there is neither adversary nor misfortune.

1 KINGS 5:4

OH, HOW WONDERFUL IT IS to rest in you, my Lord! There is no greater peace than the peace you have placed in my heart. I'm ready to celebrate your glorious birth because my life is firmly resting in your hands.

Jesus came to establish peace within our hearts; we must refuse to allow the celebration of his coming to replace that peace with stress and anxiety.

December 24

On entering the house, [the wise men] saw the child with Mary his mother; and they knelt down and paid him homage. Then, opening their treasure chests, they offered him gifts of gold, frankincense, and myrrh.

MATTHEW 2:11

HEAVENLY FATHER, when you sent Jesus, you gave your best to us. As I consider how to go about emulating that kind of love this season, I'd like to give in a significant way to someone who is in need. There are many, many opportunities to give, but I'd like to do more than just buy a present; I'd like to give myself. Please show me how and show me who. Bring your joy to the giving. Thank you, heavenly Father!

And [Mary] gave birth to her firstborn son and wrapped him in bands of cloth, and laid him in a manger, because there was no place for them in the inn.

LUKE 2:7

MY DEAR LORD, I celebrate this very special day when you came as a baby. Help me be not like those busy inns, which had no room for you. Indeed, I want you to be in the center of my home and in my heart. I want to praise you and honor you with my gifts. Just as you are the Supreme Giver, I want to return to you a gift of my own—my heart. This I pray. Amen.

Those who make room in their hearts for Christ find his company so exquisitely joyful that they can't help but pity the ancient innkeeper's unwitting loss.

December 26

Turn my heart to your decrees, and not to selfish gain. Turn my eyes from looking at vanities; give me life in your ways.

PSALM 119:36–37

*L*ORD, PLEASE BRING this truth home to my heart today: that the essence of Christmas is love—your love reaching us and setting our hearts aglow with love for you and for all people. Let love rule this day after Christmas. Let love rule my heart. Help me enjoy living successfully in your wonderful love.

How many observe Christ's birthday! How few, his precepts! O! 'tis easier to keep holidays than commandments.

—BENJAMIN FRANKLIN, POOR RICHARD'S ALMANACK

And we have seen and do testify that the Father has sent his Son as the Savior of the world.... So we have known and believe the love that God has for us.

1 JOHN 4:14, 16

$\mathcal{B}$ABY OF BETHLEHEM,
born among humble men,
cared for and shared with them;
you help me see
this is God's sympathy,
shown unreservedly
for all in poverty—
even for me....

—MICHAEL JOHN RADFORD COUNSELL

**Don't forget to receive God's gift
of grace to you; he bought it and
wrapped it himself.**

December 28

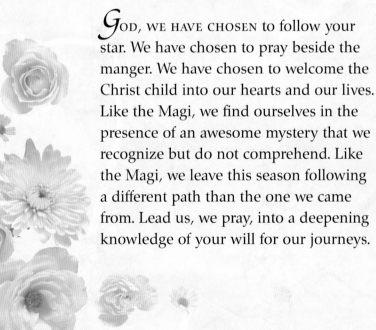

*And having been warned in a dream not to return to
Herod, they left for their own country by another road.*

MATTHEW 2:12

GOD, WE HAVE CHOSEN to follow your
star. We have chosen to pray beside the
manger. We have chosen to welcome the
Christ child into our hearts and our lives.
Like the Magi, we find ourselves in the
presence of an awesome mystery that we
recognize but do not comprehend. Like
the Magi, we leave this season following
a different path than the one we came
from. Lead us, we pray, into a deepening
knowledge of your will for our journeys.

December 29

In my anguish I cried to the Lord, and he answered by setting me free. The Lord is with me; I will not be afraid. What can man do to me?

PSALM 118:5–6, NIV

WE ARE EXCEEDINGLY GRATEFUL, O Lord, for You have heard our cries and complaints, and You responded with mercy and strength. Now our lives are overflowing with thanksgiving, and our mouths are filled with Your praises. You have not always shielded us from the pains of trouble or the ravages of conflict, but You have kept us even in the midst of sorrow and suffering. Thus we know You will fulfill Your purposes in our lives. Your love and mercy is everlasting.

—LESLIE F. BRANDT

Life is far too short to spend too much time worrying.

December 30

O SWEET AND LOVING GOD,
When I stay asleep too long,
Oblivious to all your many blessings,
Then, please, wake me up,
And sing to me your joyful song.
It is a song without noise or notes.
It is a song of love beyond words,
Of faith beyond the power of human telling.
I can hear it in my soul,
When you awaken me to your presence.

—MECHTHILD OF MAGDEBURG

**To have my first thought be of
God when I awake is to begin
my day divinely.**

December 31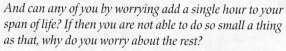

And can any of you by worrying add a single hour to your span of life? If then you are not able to do so small a thing as that, why do you worry about the rest?

LUKE 12:25–26

THE CALENDAR IS AS BARE as the Christmas tree; the page of tomorrow is clean and ready. Heavenly Father, please bless the New Year that beckons, helping us face what we must, celebrate every triumph we can, and make the changes we need to make. And now we praise you to the fullest during this horn-blowing, toast-raising moment, for it is the threshold between the old and new us. Amen.

My prayer life:

_____

_____

_____

_____

_____

_____

_____

_____

_____

_____

_____

ACKNOWLEDGMENTS

Publications International, Ltd., has made every effort to locate the owners of all copyrighted material to obtain permission to use the selections that appear in this book. Any errors or omissions are unintentional; corrections, if necessary, will be made in future editions.

Jan. 11: "The Wire Fence" from *Prayers* by Michel Quoist. Copyright © 1963 by Sheed & Ward. Reprinted by permission of Sheed & Ward, an Apostolate of the Priests of the Sacred Heart. 7373 S. Lover's Lane Rd., Franklin, WI 53132.

Jan. 14: From *Strengthening Your Grip: Essentials in an Aimless World* by Charles R. Swindoll. Copyright © 1982 by Charles R. Swindoll. Reprinted by permission of Word Publishing, Nashville, TN. All rights reserved.

Jan. 17, Sept. 29: From *Søren Kierkegaard's Journals and Papers*, edited by Edward V. Hong and Edna H. Hong. Copyright © 1970, 1976, 1978 by Indiana University Press. Reprinted by permission of Indiana University Press, Bloomington & Indianapolis.

Jan. 23, Feb. 6: Prayers by Reinhold Niebuhr. Reprinted by permission of the estate of Reinhold Niebuhr.

Feb. 27, Oct. 10: From *The Prayers of Peter Marshall*, compiled and edited by Catherine Marshall. Copyright © 1949, 1950, 1951, 1954 by Catherine Marshall. Copyright © renewed 1982 by Catherine Marshall. Reprinted by permission of Fleming H. Revell, a division of Baker Book House Company.

March 15: "My Friend" from *Prayers* by Michel Quoist. Copyright © 1963 by Sheed & Ward. Reprinted by permission of Sheed & Ward, an Apostolate of the Priests of the Sacred Heart. 7373 S. Lover's Lane Rd., Franklin, WI 53132.

March 23, April 2, 14: From *Diamonds in the Dust* by Joni Eareckson Tada. Copyright © 1993 by Joni Eareckson Tada. Reprinted by permission of Zondervan Publishing House.

March 25, Dec. 2: From *Guide My Feet* by Marian Wright Edelman. Copyright © 1995 by Marian Wright Edelman. Reprinted by permission of Beacon Press, Boston.

March 26: From *A Burden Shared* by Jane Kirkpatrick. Copyright © 1998 by Jane Kirkpatrick. Reprinted by permission of Multnomah Publishers, Inc.

April 13: From *Riches Stored in Secret Places* by Verdell Davis. Copyright © 1994 by Verdell Davis. Reprinted by permission of Word Publishing, Nashville, TN. All rights reserved.

April 20, July 8, 22: From *Power Praying: Prayer that Produces Results* by Jennifer Kennedy Dean. Copyright © 1997 by Jennifer Kennedy Dean. Reprinted by permission of the author.

May 4, 16, 30: From *15 Minutes Alone with God for Men* by Bob Barnes. Copyright © 1995 by Harvest House Publishers. Reprinted by permission of Harvest House Publishers, Eugene, OR 97402.

May 26: From *Knowing God* by J. I. Packer. Copyright © 1973 by J. I. Packer. Reprinted by permission of InterVarsity Press, Downers Grove, IL. All rights reserved.

June 2, 25: From *Silence on Fire* by William H. Shannon. Copyright © 1991 by William H. Shannon. Reprinted by permission of The Crossroad Publishing Company.

June 4, 19: From *Love Affair: A Prayer Journal* by Andrew M. Greeley. Copyright © 1992 by Andrew M. Greeley. Reprinted by permission of The Crossroad Publishing Company.

June 8: "O, God, You Conceived Us," a poem from *Naked Before God* by Bill Williams with Martha Williams. Copyright © 1998 by William P. and Martha S. Williams. Reprinted by permission of Morehouse Publishing, Harrisburg, PA.

June 14: Reprinted by permission of Heidi Waldrop Bay.

June 18: Copyright © 1970 by Fred M. Rogers. Reprinted by permission of Family Communications, Inc.

June 23: From "Great Is Thy Faithfulness," by Thomas O. Chisholm. Copyright © 1923. Renewal 1951 Hope Publishing Co. Reprinted by permission of Hope Publishing Co., Carol Stream, IL, 60188.